Paul Tonks

The Pocket Essential

FILM MUSIC

www.pocketessentials.com

First published in Great Britain 2001 by Pocket Essentials, 18 Coleswood Road, Harpenden, Herts, AL5 1EQ

Distributed in the USA by Trafalgar Square Publishing, PO Box 257, Howe Hill Road, North Pomfret, Vermont 05053

A CIP catalogue record for this book is available from the British Library.

ISBN 1-903047-63-3

2 4 6 8 10 9 7 5 3 1

Book typeset by Pdunk
Printed and bound by Cox & Wyman

for Rebecca, my "confoundedly attractive woman"

Acknowledgements

Glen Aitken, Steve Bartek, Jonathan Broxton, James Cox, Paul Duncan, Keiron Earnshaw, Robin Esterhammer, Michael Giacchino, Rudy Koppl, Ian Lace, Geoff Leonard, Paul Lewis, Dick Lewzey, Carl Ogawa, Matthew Peerless, Steve Race, Deanne Scott, Elliot Thorpe, Robert Townson, Michael Voigt, Mark Walker, Debbie Wiseman, the British Academy Of Composers And Songwriters, Garrett Axford Public Relations And Marketing, Mum, Dad and all the directors/composers who have inspired my writing.

"As much to the crew of the Enterprise, I owe you my thanks."

CONTENTS

1. You Ain't Heard Nothing Yet

Whether you're someone who has just begun discovering film music, someone obliged to learn more for educational purposes or a long-standing geek fan, this book is respectfully yours. Compiled here is an introduction to the film composer's craft in chronological order. Each chapter takes a period in history, namechecks the writers who made a difference and observes what was happening in the industry for a difference to be warranted and possible. The names go by pretty fast, but hopefully with cross-referencing and album recommendations at the end, the most important ones stay in the memory.

With that disclaimer in place – what is film music? Whenever music is written to support something else it is called 'applied' as opposed to 'pure.' So its categorisation as 'applied music' helps give a literal answer. For our purpose, a more specific definition is that it is music applied to support the action of a theatrically released film. New songs are written, old ones are reused, classical pieces are quoted from, and sometimes the sound effects themselves are deemed music. All of these will be mentioned in context, but it's the work of the film composer that this book concentrates on.

Begin by asking yourself the following questions: what makes the title scroll of a *Star Wars* movie exciting? Why is the tiny dot of a camel in vast desert sands so beautiful in *Lawrence Of Arabia*? What's so frightening about a delivery van appearing on the horizon at the end of *Se7en*? Why is Scarlett O'Hara's sunset silhouette so heartbreaking in *Gone With The Wind*? Why do we jump when Sydney opens an empty closet door in *Scream*? In *Vertigo*, how do we know that Madeleine is going to throw herself out the tower window and that Scotty won't be able to save her? The answer to each is, of course, thanks to the music. The composers manipulate our emotions and intuitive understanding for these illustrative moments. By whatever method it is realised, film music is the unseen narrative voice communicating everything we need to feel. It can duplicate, contradict, or even act regardless of the action and dialogue. Take it away, and by its absence it is missed.

That said, it's a curious fact that most audiences are never aware of a film's music. Light may travel faster than sound, but does that excuse people's general reaction of not recalling any music if asked? This is the main reason for an ongoing disregard for the film composer's art. To this can be added disdain from the classical realm for not being 'pure,' and it being ignored by the ever-changing pop music world because it remains primarily orchestral. With so much combined ignorance, it's a wonder it stayed popular in the industry. Yet there are more orchestral scores being written and being released on album today than there ever have been.

Another curious fact about contemporary audiences is that 90% leave the cinema (or stop the video/DVD) as soon as the end credits begin to roll. Unless there's a rare continuation of footage or some bloopers, no one's interested in a list of names with musical backing. It used to be that composers were given this time for a score suite. This time is now generally given to song placement. For *Titanic* (1997), the biggest ever cinematic and film music success story, that time went to 'My Heart Will Go On.' *Titanic*'s album sold over 25 million copies worldwide, and the song stayed at Number 1 in US charts for sixteen weeks. The discrepancies here are how could a score be so popular if it wasn't generally noticed, and how could a song do so well if few stayed in their seats to hear Celine Dion? Since a large proportion of sales accrued prior to the film's release, the answer comes down to how the marketing-oriented industry works today. To understand that properly, we have to journey back before the real-life ocean liner even set sail.

The Rest Is Silents

Uncertainty about applying sound to film dates back to the beginnings of cinema, before the technology was available to make use of it. Musical accompaniment preceded the first 'talkie' by a number of years. After the Lumière brothers set the wheels of a new industry in motion with footage of a steam engine (1895), fickle audiences wanted an increasing amount of spectacle. Longer pieces of film begat an entire storyline with *The Great Train Robbery* (1903). Around that time it became common to have a piano improvising to what was on screen (and neatly hiding the clanking projector noise). Even though classicist Camille Saint-Saëns was commissioned to provide a score for *L'Assassinat du Duc de Guise* (1908), it was the 20s before a music-publishing clerk named Max Winkler devised a short-lived system of providing pianists with cue sheets of existing pieces. Simultaneous to that taking effect, the major Hollywood studios began spending vast sums of money experimenting with sound technologies.

Warner Brothers used the Vitaphone system to synchronise a sound disc of rudimentary effects to their premiere of *Don Juan* (1926). History records an audience reaction that was casually indifferent to the experience. Hence the following year, the studios signed the Big Five Agreement to delay the introduction of synchronised sound until they agreed on one system and were confident of its usefulness. Fortunately they were almost immediately reassured on all counts. Mere months later, Warner again made history with the words "You ain't heard nothing yet" bursting from Al Jolson in *The Jazz Singer* (1927). It was a straightforward demonstration of simple microphone placement, but it laid down the gauntlet for the industry. While directors like Alfred Hitchcock languished in attempts to hide recording equipment in flowerpots for *Blackmail* (1929), the idea of a fully synchronised 'talkie' was suddenly possible and desirable. It seems inconceivable today that Leonardo DiCaprio and Kate Winslet might have been left mouthing sweet nothings while a screencard interrupted to announce: "Iceberg, roight ahead!"

Classical pieces were the easiest musical application with sound technology in place. At the start of Universal's reign of horror greats, Bela Lugosi's *Dracula* (1931) benefited from the soulful strains of Tchaikovsky's 'Swan Lake.' Some studios went a step further and asked contemporary classical composers to write pieces to be added later. Stravinsky and Holst both worked on scores that never saw the light of day, but Shostakovich graduated from years as an improvising pianist to being asked to write something to perform with *New Babylon* (1929). Then he fully scored *Alone* (1930), which was his native Russia's first sound film.

The real turning point in film music history came courtesy of Austrian-born Max Steiner, affectionately dubbed the 'Father of Film Music.' He arrived in Hollywood at the end of a streak of Musicals, which were one way the industry had embraced the use of sound. At the start of the 30s there was still a commonly held concern that cinema audiences wouldn't understand where a full musical underscore would be coming from. It took the bravery of RKO producer David O Selznick to get over it and instruct Steiner to compose one for *Symphony Of Six Million* (1932). The groundbreaking result shook those notions apart and almost immediately led to the creation of musical departments within the major studios. As resident musical director of RKO for several years (before moving onto Warners), Steiner had his pick of projects. It was his *King Kong* (1933) that signified the dawn of a new era. Whenever thanked by admirers for inventing film music, Steiner would brush compliments away and point them in the direction of late German romantic composer Richard Wagner (whose work had appeared in film as early as 1915 with *The Birth Of A*

Nation). In his opinion Wagner would have been the foremost film composer. All of which is in reference to the leitmotif – the idea of linking the appearances of a person, place or thing together with a recurring musical phrase. It may seem commonplace and common sense today, but for film it began with *King Kong*. The ape's three-note motif is as simple an idea as John Williams would later create for *Jaws*. We feel and fear his presence when not actually on screen because of this motif. We suspend disbelief for the stop-motion puppets because of its power and nobility. Its importance for this film, and the craft, from then on cannot be stressed enough. It gave licence for the opening of a film to feature a musical overture introducing principal themes. It also meant a brief reprise could accompany the audience's exit, back in a Golden Age when there were no long lists of names to read.

2. The Golden Age

The Golden Age is one of several terms bandied about without anyone really bothered with defining what it means, when it started, when it ended, or why. Quite often the term seems to be a way for an elder to tell us everything used to be so much rosier in their day, and tough luck you weren't there to experience it. Where film music is concerned, it romantically means a period when its craft matched the artistry of the films themselves, unsullied by commercialism or committee decision-making. That period arguably starts at Steiner's *King Kong* with its intellectualised methods. It had an immediately obvious influence on how scores were written. Naturally, everything that previously falls into the Silent film category should be separated from the definition, but chronologically this ignores much that shouldn't be forgotten. Worthies include the previously mentioned Musicals, the works of Edmund Meisel on *The Battleship Potemkin* (1925) and *October* (1927), and even the encapsulation of American good humour despite the Depression Era in Charlie Chaplin's sketched and hummed tunes for the likes of *City Lights* (1931). These all contributed to the styles and approaches of later works. If *King Kong* is to be taken as the starting point however, then it's the richly dramatic style that distinguishes itself from what came before. The Golden Age is easier to pinpoint by concentrating on this style because like all fashions, it only stayed popular for so long.

Steiner went on to produce some of the most memorable film scores in history. He put thunder under the hooves of *The Charge Of The Light Brigade* (1936), and a golden glow of emotional beauty and fortitude behind Tara's life story in *Gone With The Wind* (1939). Later he became inextricably linked to the best of Humphrey Bogart's career during the popularity of film noir. *The Big Sleep* (1946), *The Treasure Of The Sierra Madre* (1948) and *Key Largo* (1948) are all scores that sustain the classic image of Bogart as everybody's favourite gangster/gumshoe. Steiner's contribution to *Casablanca* (1942) demonstrates just how powerful a tool film music can be. 'As Time Goes By' was actually written by Herman Hupfeld for a Broadway show a decade earlier, but Steiner's integration of the melody into his underscore makes it inseparable from the film. The result is a leitmotif that acts as a snapshot of a time, place, character, mood and range of emotions that's instantly recognisable and endlessly spoofable.

All things being equal, Steiner was not averse to being influenced himself of course. With *The Adventures Of Don Juan* (1949) we find the real core of what's considered Golden Age music. In Errol Flynn, Hollywood discovered and developed one of the first Superstars. One word sums up the music and the man: swashbuckle. You'll often hear about Golden Age film composers, and this refers to anything up to a dozen names. Steiner can be seen to have been an influence, courtesy of Flynn's career, in the style instigated by fellow Viennese composer Erich Wolfgang Korngold.

Captain Blood (1935) launched Korngold's and Flynn's careers and also initiated a new generation of adventure epics. His style, characterised by furiously fast action music dominated by brass, and achingly bitter-sweet love themes dominated by strings, still has far-reaching repercussions in the industry. It's a robust statement of regal grandeur combined with passionate romance (in both senses). *The Adventures Of Robin Hood* (1938), *The Private Lives Of Elizabeth And Essex* (1939) and *The Sea Hawk* (1940) all carry the style. When John Williams was asked for a particular sound in the 70s, it would be to these films that director George Lucas would turn for inspiration. Place the main titles of Korngold's *King's Row* (1942) next to *Star Wars* (1977), and you have one of the most obvious examples of stylistic inheritance. When you consider how much the *Star Wars* trilogy has in turn influenced cinematic trends, Korngold's significance should be very apparent. The amazing thing is he only scored a total of 16 films, yet these core swashbucklers affected the careers of every composer who followed suit. Whether asked to or not…

Alfred Newman worked on many costume epics in an enormous career spanning almost 250 scores. In the immediate wake of the adventure epic's popularity he produced *The Mark Of Zorro* (1940), *Song Of Fury* (1942), *The Black Swan* (1942), *Captain From Castile* (1947) and *Prince Of Foxes* (1949) to name only a few. Apart from sustaining the symphonic sound, Newman is also responsible for something else to which *Star Wars* owes a debt of thanks. His 20th Century-Fox fanfare has never seemed more at home than in preceding the space trilogy. It was composed during his period as head of the studio's music department. Like Steiner at RKO, the position involved collating composers, instrumentalists, orchestrators and technicians together all under one roof. All this was in addition to writing his own scores. Something in his string writing often suggested a religious spirituality, although he was in fact a non-practising Jew. In conducting, he would encourage a great deal of expression and vibrato (exaggerated wobble) in the string performances. His score to *The Song Of Bernadette* (1943) came after a long line of successful works where this particular sound can be heard, such as: *The Prisoner Of Zenda* (1937), *The Hurricane* (1937), *Wuthering Heights* (1939), *The Hunchback Of Notre Dame* (1939) and *How Green Was My Valley* (1941). With *Bernadette* however came a turning point that touched many things simultaneously.

Researching the important scene of a vision of the Virgin Mary, Newman hit upon the epitomy of his impressionistic style. As opposed to Steiner's more specific leitmotifs, Newman instead drew from the mood and requirements of scenes. The result of the impressions coming together for this score was an Academy Award, and something almost completely unheard of even as late as the 40s: an album of the dramatic underscore. Up to this point, it wasn't possible for anyone to be a soundtrack collector. The vinyl format and charts had been around for some years, but it was rare to see anything film-related appearing on either. Some vague notion of using popular songs in unison with a movie had begun in the Silent era. The notion grew with the success of Disney's *Snow White And The Seven Dwarves* (1938), which had an album of its singalong songs. Disney would also be the first to call an album an Original Soundtrack with *Pinocchio* (1940). Yet nothing until this point actually deserved that title, because they were all new recordings and not taken from what was used in the film itself. *The Song Of Bernadette* was an important indication that there was a public demand for film music on record.

Another of Newman's legacies is the family he left to carry on the good work. Brothers Emil and Lionel became Hollywood composers, with the latter taking over as Head of Fox Music when Alfred moved on. Working today are his two sons David (*Bill And Ted's Excellent Adventure*, *Galaxy Quest*) and Thomas (*The Shawshank Redemption*, *American Beauty*), and his nephew Randy (*The Natural*, *Toy Story*).

Others Who Polished The Gold

Although stylistically it's often thought Victor Young only peripherally belonged among the Golden Age greats, that's at the cost of ignoring a great gift for melody and an understanding of commercial potential. He was another to pioneer the possibilities of soundtracks on vinyl by re-recording his dramatic underscore to *For Whom The Bell Tolls* (1943). His career took off when he was snapped up by Paramount Studios after recording pieces for silent movies. He stayed with them for a lifetime.

Melodic highlights there included *The Uninvited* (1944) and *Samson And Delilah* (1949). Elsewhere, *Rio Grande* (1950) and especially *Shane* (1952) were at the forefront of the Western genre of the day.

In slightly higher regard is Hugo Friedhofer. His technical excellence was often sought out - by Alfred Newman to score pictures at Fox, and by Korngold and Steiner to assist orchestrating their work. In between these assignments, he thankfully found time to apply his wonderful ability for harmonic invention and stark coloration to scores of his own. Starting in 1937 with *The Adventures Of Marco Polo* (another swashbuckler), notables include: *The Lodger* (1944), *Broken Arrow* (1950), *Seven Cities Of Gold* (1955), *The Sun Also Rises* (1957) and *This Earth Is Mine* (1959). Without doubt, *The Best Years Of Our Lives* (1946) is Friedhofer's greatest achievement. Apart from public favour and winning an Oscar, it's to be acknowledged for being the first time a film score was well received by general music critics. That's not to say it changed their elitist opinions forever, but it is another indication that the Golden Age style had the power to affect and influence much around it.

Like Korngold before him, German composer Franz Waxman found himself persuaded to find safer haven in Hollywood with the imminent outbreak of World War II. Almost immediately he had an enormous effect on the industry with his grandiose score to *The Bride Of Frankenstein* (1935). Waxman's intuitive thinking behind the score shines through. Using the ondes martenot instrument (similar to the theremin - see below), he gave an original and peculiar atmosphere to the doomed romance. The orchestra performed in an impressionistic way to double the sounds of the strange laboratory equipment. There had been sequel movies and scores before (Steiner was rushed into delivering *Son Of Kong* in 1933), but none had the same degree of success and respect. Many more would follow, and the Universal studio dutifully took its monster-movie series into overdrive. Universal also rewarded Waxman with a two-year contract as music director. He then skipped to MGM for another seven-year contract (and later Warner Brothers) as one of several resident composers.

The Waxman sound echoes the Golden Age because it is full of brass fanfares, and has a languorous softness to his romantic themes. He had tremendous success with *Sunset Boulevard* (1950), *A Place In The Sun* (1951), delving into derring-do with *Prince Valiant* (1954) and into sexual repression with *Peyton Place* (1957). A strong indication of the man's ability is that the classics *Rebecca* and *The Philadelphia Story* were written in tandem during 1940. The former was the first of four pictures for the uniquely influential Alfred Hitchcock. *Suspicion* (1941), *The Paradine Case* (1947) and *Rear Window* (1954) all followed. Hitchcock demonstrated tremendous musical savvy throughout his career, selecting composers who were almost always perfect for the job.

The Oscar awarded to the music for *Spellbound* (1945) doesn't begin to acknowledge the achievement of Hungarian composer Miklós Rózsa. It must have been an enormous challenge being given a Hitchcock, Gregory Peck and Ingrid Bergman headliner with material tackling Freudian psychology and incorporating dream sequences designed by Salvador Dali. Nevertheless, he proved his worth to all concerned by test scoring a sequence using the theremin to depict Peck's paranoiac tendencies. The eerie wailing sound of the electronic instrument was subsequently associated with any form of cinematic psychosis. Integrated into a score that also featured a beautiful love theme, Rózsa later adapted the material into the 'Spellbound Concerto,' which has been a concert hall favourite and had many album recordings.

Rózsa actually beat both Newman's *Song Of Bernadette* and Young's *For Whom The Bell Tolls* to vinyl with *The Jungle Book*, which was re-recorded for an experimental commercial sales venture in 1942. It may not have had its original tracks, but without that experiment others would have been slower to follow. He got to make his mark at the other end of the decade anyway with the world's first complete underscore album release for *Madame Bovary* (1949). In and around these landmarks, he developed a preference for musical research and a bold opulent style with: *The Thief Of Baghdad* (1940), *That Hamilton Woman* (1941), *Double Indemnity* (1944), *The Lost Weekend* (1945) and *The Red House* (1947). These were 2 decades of prodigious achievement, but would be eclipsed by his historical and religious epics of the next 10 years.

There was a more popular moment of record industry history in 1944. Fox Studios were inundated with requests for David Raksin's music to their stylish murder mystery *Laura*. The following year, five versions of a song with newly-commissioned lyrics were in the US Top 10. It was a welcome indication that audiences could notice and appreciate a score, but the unwelcome result was a continuation of corporate thinking that the material would only sell in song format. The greater shame is that the frequently outspoken Raksin was completely against applying lyrics to his theme. One infamous tale that illustrates his philosophical and ethical nature is from Hitchcock's *Lifeboat* (1944). Originally contracted to score, his work was stopped before it started when a message from Hitch announced there would be no music. The director felt that for a film set entirely on a small boat no one would understand where the music was coming from. Raksin sent back a reply to say he'd answer that when someone explained where the cameras were. As a result, the scoring duties went to Hugo Friedhofer. Raksin's style might not necessarily have been swashbuckling enough to be Golden Age, yet *Laura*, *The Adventures Of Sherlock Holmes* (1939), *Forever Amber* (1947) and *The Bad And The Beautiful* (1952) all possess some of the most pleasingly memorable melodies of their time.

Since so much stock is placed in the Academy Awards these days, it's worth mentioning that the first Oscar ceremony took place in 1935. The Best Music, Score category was won by Victor Schertzinger and Gus Kahn for *One Night Of Love*. Schertzinger was also the film's director and his songwriting talent made a star out of Grace Moore with 'Ciri-Biri-Bin.' The film's music was largely an exercise in making popular the rarefied world of opera, so it's interesting to note how right from the start dramatic underscores were ignored by the Academy. Max Steiner was nominated for *The Lost Patrol* over a list of nearly thirty other films he worked on in the same year, and also over a similarly busy Alfred Newman. Perhaps finding its feet for a few years, the Academy gradually made amends acknowledging Steiner in 1936 (*The Informer*), Korngold in 1937 (*Anthony Adverse*) and Newman in 1939 (*Alexander's Ragtime Band*) when the category was opened out into three for Original Score, Scoring and Song.

Being a Hollywood venture, the Oscars at that time couldn't help but overlook what was happening elsewhere in the world. In England, Sir Arthur Bliss wrote what is considered a major landmark in film scoring with *Things To Come* (1936). For this first fully-realised cinematic science fiction (based on HG Wells' novel), the ambitious piece was largely written before the film was made. As such, the three 78-rpm records can't qualify as the first dramatic underscore of its kind to be released. The central 'March' was almost immediately divorced from the film anyway and became a concert hall favourite.

A similar fate often befell the scores of contemporary classicists who were cajoled, if only briefly, into the cinematic limelight. Two more English composers to make fleeting Golden Age cameos were Ralph Vaughan Williams whose *Scott Of The Antarctic* (1948) is far better known as his 'Sixth Symphony,' and Sir William Walton whose Shakespearean adaptations of *Henry V* (1943) and *Hamlet* (1947) have often been recorded and performed as concert suites. In America, Aaron Copland's directness and folk tune sensibility led to a handful of film scores that made sense of the word Americana more than any other work. *Our Town* (1940) is the quintessential portrait of small-town USA and has been emulated ever since. Brassy fanfares, simple harmonics and patriotic pride were the staples of his music for both concert stage and screen, and were the perfect fuel for the nation entering WWII (especially his non-film piece 'Fanfare For The Common Man').

Sergei Prokofiev's astonishingly powerful *Alexander Nevsky* (1938) was another example of war propaganda inspiring great cinema. Like comrade Shostakovich's earlier works though, the Russian epic wasn't widely seen in America at the time. The music became far more internationally familiar in edited form as a cantata (largely vocal work) for performance, as opposed to its intended place against director Sergei Eisenstein's awe-inspiring visuals. The 2 visionaries reunited in 1942 for the only slightly less breathtaking *Ivan The Terrible*. Prokofiev's boundlessly energetic tempos coupled with affecting use of wordless voices may have been unappreciated in its time. It has most definitely been rediscovered and paid homage to in the work of contemporary A-list Hollywood composers however. For example, several of Danny Elfman and James Horner's works are richer thanks to the pairing of Prokofiev with Eisenstein. They have had their own great composer/director relationships as we shall see later, but this was the first instance of the all too rare working method. It has always produced the very best in film music, and with no more glitteringly obvious results than in the career of one of the greatest architects of cinema's Golden Age: Bernard Herrmann.

Today the name Bernard Herrmann is almost inseparable from Alfred Hitchcock. There was well over a decade of cinema from the composer before they got together though. At the very start was a collaboration that had just as profound an effect on the industry. Herrmann had been working with Orson Welles for some time already in radio (*War Of The Worlds*) when Hollywood beckoned. Together they crafted the universally accepted masterpiece that is *Citizen Kane* (1941). Above all others, Herrmann was the one composer who transcended the Ages. No genre of film was closed to him. He would later tackle a new form of the swashbuckling adventure epic when the fantasy genre was reinvented for monster flicks featuring Ray Harryhausen's stop-motion animation such as *Jason And The Argonauts* (1963). Yet when faced with an industry almost entrenched in a uniform approach to film scoring at the start of the 40s, Herrmann typically chose to fly in the face of convention. The music of *Citizen Kane* covers newsreel pastiche, an operatic extract, a homely dialogue scene spun across a montage of years and plenty of the brooding turmoil succinctly characterising Charles Foster Kane. The film opens with an explorative journey around the castle-like Xanadu mansion. Though darkly lit, it could just be a For Sale promo were it not for the guttural brass combining with sighing and moaning woodwinds. In one fell swoop, Herrmann took the Golden Age style and applied it in a shocking new way. This was a score for atmosphere.

From the very beginnings of his career, a dark colour shaded his writing. In many of the films he is more popularly known for, this colour helped with the setting and pre-empting of atmospheres. A superb example is *Cape Fear* (1962), which was more viscerally interpreted for a modern audience in 1991 by Martin Scorsese. Elmer Bernstein adapted the original score for the new version. In both it makes for a chilling ride of terror in the 'Main Titles' alone. Dark colours were particular to Herrmann, but copied by others in characterising someone's unspoken psychological state (coining the term 'Herrmannesque'). Simplicity and economy were evident in his score pages, and as David Raksin once put it, "Benny was a genius with the repeat sign." Many of his score pages had the appearance of small cells of music endlessly falling back on themselves. None of this is to say that he revolutionised music, but he revolutionised its relationship to the screen.

Through the rest of the 40s, Herrmann worked on films that indulged both sides of his musical and private personality. His 1942 Oscar for *All That Money Can Buy* (aka *The Devil And Daniel Webster*) was the only time he was honoured by the Academy, and was really in apology for not being able to acknowledge the politically incorrect *Citizen Kane*. The project was a 19th-Century setting of the tale of Faust's pact with the devil, and this combination of psychological complexity in a historical setting suited the composer perfectly. *The Magnificent Ambersons* (1942), *Jane Eyre* (1943), *Hangover Square* (1945), *Anna And The King Of Siam* (1946) and *Portrait Of Jennie* (1948) all followed with similarly impressive results. It was *The Ghost And Mrs Muir* (1947) that became his favourite score however, and truly summed up everything Herrmann wanted to say. With the earlier *Jane Eyre* he'd found a very personal identification with a time and place. It inspired him to write his only opera (*Wuthering Heights*), and it thrilled him to be able to further apply his gothic extravagances and poetic morbidities to what was really a companion piece in the ghostly tale of Mrs Muir's Gull Cottage. There are legendary stories about Herrmann's gruff irascible manner, but none surround this project. His preoccupation with solitude and death are all realised in a lyrical backing for the romance between Gene Tierney and Rex

Harrison's sea captain from the grave. More than in any other of his scores, Herrmann makes use of the leitmotif. Galloping woodwinds pull the tides, clarinets offer nautical whimsy for Captain Gregg and strings define the doomed earthly love affair. He playfully referred to it as his "Max Steiner score," acknowledging the Golden Age style around him.

From Gold To Silver

Herrmann's role is essential to understand why the Golden Age is considered to have ended and been replaced by something else. He translated his overall personality to an art form that otherwise capitulated to a studio system set in its ways. It was enough of a change in thinking to allow bigger changes to follow.

In 1949 Columbia Records introduced the 33 1/3-rpm format onto the market, followed by the 45-rpm single from RCA Victor. Releasing fuller lengths of a full movie score was of course hampered by the 78-rpm format before this. The single was the more influential format with the new branch of pop charts it created. Anton Karas' 'Harry Lime Theme' from *The Third Man* (1949) stayed at Number 1 for eleven weeks the following year. It was an immediate indication of a change in popular and studio thinking towards film music. More pertinently, being a score from a complete unknown Viennese performer that's entirely on an equally unknown instrument (the zither), this is a bigger indication that studios (British Lion/London Films) were changing their thinking about the application of music. It's a coincidence that Orson Welles is in the film, but is it a coincidence that such a radical departure in style followed a decade of unconventional instrument combinations and applications from Herrmann?

No one score marks the end of one Age and the beginning of the next. The word Age is a little redundant or misleading in the way it's used. At the end of the 40s and beginning of the 50s, musical ideas were expanding rapidly and we basically had a transitional period. Ask someone to which era Miklós Rózsa's *Ben-Hur* or Alex North's *Cleopatra* belong and invariably it'll be to the Golden Age, yet the former was 1959 and the latter 1963. From the other perspective, ask about Karas' *Third Man* or even Herrmann's theremin-rich *The Day The Earth Stood Still* (1951), and already the waters are a little muddied because their style leans toward what is differentiated as being The Silver Age. All this therefore conforms to my suggestion that what's being referred to is a style of music as opposed to a strict time-frame.

The Golden Age style has never gone away. It has enjoyed periods of renewed favour - John Williams in the 70s, for example. With the recording industry changing, the looming advent of rock 'n' roll, and especially with television monopolising audiences, the orchestral form was politely asked to take a sidestep for others to try their hand.

3. Anything Goes

If The Golden Age was tough to describe, The Silver Age is even more so. No later Bronze Age has ever been identified, so perhaps this second era never really ended. Silver is a description of a particular area of musical style that is clearly different from Golden. The word Age is again misleading, because the distinction between the two is nothing to do with any start or stop in time. For the purposes of chapter breakdown however, it's a happy fact that this changeover happened over the course of a measurable number of years.

Moving into the 50s, several cinematic trends enjoyed a period of favour that encouraged composers to find new means of expression. Film Noir had appeared in the 40s, and as previously mentioned, Max Steiner helped Bogart immensely in that area. There were also some inventively dark-humoured scores coming out of London's Ealing Studios for *Passport To Pimlico* (Georges Auric) and *Kind Hearts And Coronets* (adapting Mozart for murder) in 1949, and later for Auric's *The Lavender Hill Mob* (1951) and Tristram Cary's *The Ladykillers* (1955). Any trend that originated from within the industry could only hope to affect small change at this time. Cinema as a whole was reeling far harder from an outside attack – the increasing popularity of television.

Experiments had been conducted all over the world, notably in the 20s by John Logie Baird in London and Charles Francis Jenkins in North America. It took until the 30s for the public to cautiously show interest. While 400 sets in the New York area were receiving broadcasts from the National Broadcasting Company (NBC) in 1939, there were many tens of thousands more in England receiving from the British Broadcasting Company (BBC). It had an enormous impact on cinema attendance. The outbreak of World War II resulted in television production in America stopping altogether and there was a temporary resurgence of interest in the big screen. A post-war economic boom 6 years later meant that sales of television sets suddenly soared. The US figures going into the 50s are truly astounding. The number of home sets went from around 7000 in 1946, to 10 million in 1950, to 22 million in 1952, then half of all American homes just one year later. Cinema attendance figures dropped in almost direct proportion. Add the fact that both CBS and NBC announced they were developing colour television at the end of the 40s, and Hollywood considered itself in serious trouble. The studios racked their brains for ways to encourage audiences back into movie theatres. Their answer remains the same to this day - to spend obscene amounts of money on bigger and bigger spectacle.

It didn't take very long to rush the technology into place, and so in 1952 *This Is Cinerama* appeared with a curved screen six times normal size. It was a travelogue of the wonders of the age, opening with a black and white miniscreen reminder of TV dimensions, and then exploding into colour for a point of view roller-coaster ride. The music was designed to be just as awe-inspiring to remind viewers how their televisions' solitary speaker paled in comparison. Original music was credited to Howard Jackson, Paul Sawtell and Roy Webb. However, Musical Director Louis Forbes had Max Steiner secretly compose the great majority of the grand and stately orchestral work. He was under contract to Warner Brothers at the time, but didn't want to miss the opportunity to work on yet another highly influential project. That same year, Universal unveiled 3-D with *Bwana Devil* – music by Victor Young. Young got to work on a broader canvas with Cecil B DeMille's Oscar-winning *The Greatest Show On Earth*, and then knocked 'em dead with *Around The World In Eighty Days*, the first film in TODD-AO 70mm.

Golden Remnants

In 1953 the real prize for innovation went to 20th Century-Fox's CinemaScope format. It won a special award Oscar for advancement in film technology, but most praiseworthy is that it wasn't just another gimmick. Fox made the decision to apply it only to films that would truly benefit from it. Premiering the gargantuan screen ratio was *The Robe*, a sumptuous retelling of Christ's life from the perspective of Richard Burton's Roman tribune. Alfred Newman's score, like *The Song Of Bernadette*, was an example of the composer treating religious subjects with absolute respect. The result is among his grandest accomplishments, with a principal theme for the crucifixion bursting with heavenly glory from chorus and orchestra. It also benefited from the new 7-track stereophonic sound system that considerably expanded what an audience could hear of an orchestra's make-up.

The Golden Age symphonic style continued because of the religious/ sword and sandal/historical costume epic genre. Other styles were encroaching, but with *The Robe* Newman was once again largely responsible for something that upped the stakes for others to follow. The industry's response was swift and overpowering – it left us with enough afternoon TV classics to literally fill a month of Sundays.

All of the Golden Age film composers tackled at least one picture from the genre after this point, but for Miklós Rózsa it became an area of career definition. *Quo Vadis* (1951) preceded the bigger screen ratios but followed several spates of historical/adventure films. The difference was he emphasised ethical considerations over historical accuracy. The following year Newman took pains to research ancient Hebraic music for *The Robe*, but for *Vadis* Rózsa obtained every possible scrap of reference material from all over the world. The Roman Empire had never been so conscientiously investigated for its music. In doing so, he effectively created a brand new sound which 50 years later defines a time and place as believably as any that is lost to us. Full of hymns and fanfares, it was a blueprint for method and style carried through all that followed of his own (and many others') work.

He continued practising the methodology with *Ivanhoe* (1952). 12th-Century sources were equally hard to come by, yet he managed to perform a similar miracle in defining the Saxons and Normans for some thrilling battle scenes. Then it was back to the Senate for *Julius Caesar* (1953), which he chose to interpret in Elizabethan terms like a contemporary stage production of Shakespeare's play. Then back-to-back in 1956 came 16th-Century romance for King Henry II in *Diane*, and an easier to research background for the 19th-Century life of Vincent Van Gogh in *Lust For Life*. All of these applied Rózsa's Golden Age thinking, but in the eyes of enthusiasts of the craft they merely paved the way for what is inarguably one of the most important scores of all time – *Ben-Hur* (1959).

For nearly a decade the industry had been building toward staging something on the scale of this *Tale Of The Christ*. Just shy of 4 hours long, the film employed 50,000 actors, constructed an eighteen-acre set, appeared in a ratio wider than anything seen before and succeeded in rescuing M-G-M Studios from bankruptcy. Rózsa laboured for an incredible year and a half on the score, which is on as epic a scale as the movie. There are half a dozen marches, endless fanfares for stages of the chariot race, a magnificent Christ theme utilising pipe organ, powerfully strident music for Roman might and softer Jewish material for Judah Ben-Hur's love story with Esther. So many sequences illustrate the very best that music can do for a film. There's an example of 'Mickey-Mousing' (caricaturing something in music) with a musical portrait of a galley ship accelerating to ramming speed. The Christ theme is used to remind us of Him when He isn't there, draw comparisons with Charlton Heston when

He offers him water (mirroring an earlier event), and even act as His voice when distance prevents us from hearing Him give the Sermon from the Mount. For all these reasons and many more, Rózsa fully deserved his Oscar among the unprecedented eleven won by the film.

It is the best represented of all film scores on record (in all formats), and that has aided its reputation enormously. Its influence is to be admired with some awe too. Several extracts were adapted into hymns for church choir, and there are endless examples of derivative fanfares and marches used for sporting events and processional occasions. Within the industry, it stands alongside the heroic scores of Korngold as being most influential when anyone wants to elicit regal splendour or military might. Once again we can skip ahead to *Star Wars* and see stylistic comparisons. In *The Phantom Menace* (1999), the comparison of Williams' 'Flag Parade' with Rózsa's 'Parade Of The Charioteers' is unmistakable - George Lucas was specifically emulating *Ben-Hur*, one of his favourite movies, after all.

The 50s were a decade of luxury for Rózsa in allowing him to indulge in historical research. So it's not surprising he subsequently considered it a mistake to immediately follow *Ben-Hur* with *King Of Kings* (1961), which covered similar territory. The score is nevertheless a rich work of Greco-Roman melodies, with fourteen themes composed in just a few weeks! It works almost in tandem with his other popular Heston epic from the same year – *El Cid*. Culminating in *The Last Days Of Sodom And Gomorrah* (1962), this was a period of enormous output for the composer. The historical epic has never attained such heights since.

Rózsa's tale has taken us beyond the Silver Age starting point, but we can return to it by pausing at one more sword and sandal extravaganza from the end of the decade. *Spartacus* (1960) was director Stanley Kubrick's contribution to the genre and was every bit as spectacularly oversized as those that preceded it. The schizophrenic score from Alex North is considered another of the finest ever written for film (and in fan opinion is a close cousin to his *Cleopatra* of 1963), and also happens to be the all-time favourite of Steven Spielberg. Alternating between metallic and staccato (short separate bursts) rhythmic marches and a bittersweet three-note love theme, it's a work that collides intricate complexity with delicate simplicity. Depicting the barbarism of the gladiatorial ring, North uses percussion to show the same emotional detachment as the arena onlookers. It demonstrates the sort of intellectual process that had attracted him to Kubrick, and by which we can travel back a decade to pinpoint one of the clear indications of film music entering its Silver Age.

The Sound Of Silver

Since at the start of the 50s studios felt that large-screen costume dramas were not always guaranteed to make their money back, they also went for smaller black and white dramas. Stage play adaptations were a more viable financial venture, and were a desirable contrast in bringing the theatre's edge of realism and social themes to cinema. Sometimes budget was kept down by the self-contained format of something like *Twelve Angry Men* (1957), which didn't need expansive sets or music cues. Where possible, studios wanted to replicate the substantial success of Arthur Miller's *Death Of A Salesman* (1951), which North scored for both stage and screen. When director Elia Kazan decided to adapt Tennessee Williams' *A Streetcar Named Desire* that same year, there was no one better qualified to figure out how to interpret the explosive lives of Kowalski, Stella and Blanche. Jazz was North's answer. New Orleans jazz was a wholly Americanised method completely alien to cinemagoers' ears. Composer Jerry Goldsmith (who later befriended North) said, "To me when I first heard it, it was the pivotal point in film music where it all changed. Music had been totally European. Late 19th Century, early 20th Century European. French and German in style. All of a sudden it became very American. What Alex wrote was very original and his own style, successfully fusing elements of jazz and symphonic writing. There was no question that it pushed the envelope harmonically and stylistically. It was revolutionary. In the mid-50s film music definitely came of age stylistically."

As of this point, younger composers came to call him "The Boss"! Their respect is founded on far more than *A Streetcar Named Desire* saying it was okay to use jazz if you wanted. It made everyone realise that anything was possible. North continued to prove it by capturing the morbid sense of fatality in the 1952 adaptation of *Les Misérables*, his Mexican rhythms for *Viva Zapata!* the same year, and depicting chilling homicidal tendencies in a young boy for *The Bad Seed* (1956). None of this should ignore his more melodic achievements of course. Chief of which is *Unchained* (1955) whose theme went on to be a hit for The Righteous Brothers a decade later (and again for the supernatural romance of *Ghost* (1990)).

One of the younger composers happily liberated by the example of *A Streetcar Named Desire* was Leonard Rosenman. In 1955, the first year of his career, he produced three scores of significant impact. The first was *East Of Eden*, which came about when Rosenman's piano student, James

Dean, recommended him to director Kazan. To characterise adolescent angst, the composer employed dissonance (playing notes that don't quite harmonise together) and atonality (off-key notes). It became a mark of his general writing style, but here in its first full use in a film score the effect is striking. He followed this with a score for *Rebel Without A Cause*, which has similar storyline concerns, and he added a bluesy folk element to play up the tragedy. Then came *The Cobweb*, a tale of patients in a private mental clinic who seem saner than their doctors. Rosenman opted to play a similar reversal of the norm with a 12-tone atonal score. This complex method of predetermining a limited range of tone and pitch was quite a shock to the Hollywood system. By the end of the decade when Duke Ellington laced American jazz into *Anatomy Of A Murder* (1959), audiences were welcoming these new sounds openly.

Elmer Bernstein was another composer to have his career kick-started by these years of increasing open-mindedness. *The Man With The Golden Arm* (1955) is regarded as a landmark in jazz scoring. The previously taboo subject of drug addiction had no precedent in music, but the spare use of lyrical jazz rhythms (coupled with Frank Sinatra being the junkie) was enough of a softening effect for it not to be too offensive for the time. The following year, Bernstein found himself with a different challenge when he was passed the genre baton to carry for Cecil B DeMille's religious epic *The Ten Commandments*.

Silver On Record

Bernstein's *The Man With The Golden Arm* was released as a full album and stayed in the charts for several weeks. The idea that cinema could support, promote and benefit from popular music was extremely desirable for the studios. Still feeling the effect of television, they were keen to try any method of recouping costs. (Especially since bigger screen formats were potentially only of short-lasting interest to viewers constantly awaiting the next technological development.) One thing pricking up theirs' and everyone else's ears was the advent of rock 'n' roll. Chroniclers even cite the beginnings in some part attributable to cinema. When Bill Haley And The Comets released '(We're Gonna) Rock Around The Clock' in 1954 it hardly made an impact. When it appeared in the titles of *The Blackboard Jungle* the following year however, there were riots of enthusiasm in theatre auditoriums. It hit the Number 1 position immediately, spawned a movie named after the song, and a whole sub-genre devoted to teens swept up by the craze. This was also the year the RCA label introduced stereo to vinyl recordings.

Hollywood had paid attention to all the phases of pop music and its commercial possibilities. Since the Silent era there'd been one-off examples of a film song finding an extra lease of life on radio and record. As far back as 1928 people were caught unawares by the success of *Ramona*, whose title song (a waltz for the tale of racial prejudice) wound up with four cover versions simultaneously in American charts. Just prior to the rock 'n' roll explosion, United Artists had a taste of the larger exploitative potential with Russian composer Dimitri Tiomkin's *High Noon* (1952). Thanks to a delay in opening the film, the ballad he'd written completed its record negotiations and was released in advance. A pair of versions retained the film title, but throughout the picture the ballad is better known as 'Do Not Forsake Me, Oh My Darling.' This was the first successful example of a movie being promoted by a song. It was also the first time one was used so frequently and prominently in a film. Almost every time Gary Cooper strolls along the town street it seems to be filtering out of someone's window. The lyrics and mournful tone are a constant reminder that the 90-minute running time is all he has before an inevitable shoot-out to the death. Tiomkin worked within the time-frame and general style of a Golden Age composer, but his philosophy belonged very much to the Silver Age.

After winning two Oscars for *High Noon* (Song and Score), Tiomkin subsequently won 2 years later for the character study on a crashing plane that was *The High And The Mighty*. At the Award ceremony, he boldly announced, "I would like to thank Beethoven, Brahms, Wagner, Strauss, Rimsky-Korsakov..." Anyone else on that list was lost to the sound of uproarious laughter from the audience. This was a considerable faux pas as far as his contemporaries were concerned. Classical purists were offered an unintended indication they were right all along and film music just plundered the classics. It was just plain speaking, not arrogance on Tiomkin's part. In all aspects of his career he demonstrated it by being a canny self-promoter and businessman. Earlier successes included romantic and whimsical scores for Frank Capra's films *Lost Horizon* (1937), *Mr Smith Goes To Washington* (1939) and *It's A Wonderful Life* (1946). He also scored four of Hitchcock's films, namely: *Shadow Of A Doubt* (1943), *Strangers On A Train* (1951), *I Confess* (1953) and *Dial M For Murder* (1954). Later still, he would have the dubious honour of scoring what would be the last of the sword and sandal epics with the appropriately named *The Fall Of The Roman Empire* (1964). His other epics were too early or inappropriate for marketing, like his first epic scale Western, *Duel In The Sun* (1946). Unable to turn down a project, Tiomkin had a lasting association with the Western genre. *Red River* (1948) followed, then *High Noon*, *The Big Sky* (1952), *Gunfight At The OK Corral* (1957), *Rio Bravo* (1959), *The Alamo* (1960) and the immensely popular *Rawhide* TV series theme. Through all these, his catchy melodies with unexpected rhythms (and cross-rhythms) shine through, and wherever a single or album was possible he'd pursue it tenaciously.

High Noon changed Hollywood producers' ideas and motivations about the commercial viability of movie-related music. They began asking composers to craft marketable songs regardless of whether or not one was suitable for the film. A song on radio before a film's release was great promotion. It only cost a little money to make a lot, so who cared if the song had little to do with the film? It would take a few more years for this new philosophy to take hold. Thankfully there was plenty more going on in the mid-50s for composers not to be overly concerned about it.

Big-screen adaptations of Broadway Musicals were suddenly popular again, having had only marginal success since the untoppable *The Wizard Of Oz* (1939). It was another way that the studios tried the speculate-to-accumulate approach to win back viewers lost to TV. This was a reassurance that music was an important part of at least one genre of film, and often the name of one of the composers already mentioned would be hidden away in the arrangement credits, such as David Raksin on *The Harvey Girls* (1946) and Alfred Newman on *South Pacific*. The big record album successes of the decade were *Oklahoma!* and *The King And I* in 1956, and *Gigi* alongside *South Pacific* in 1958. This chapter's title, *Anything Goes* takes its name from the 1956 Bing Crosby film of Cole Porter's earlier Broadway show incidentally.

Silver From Outer Space

Another genre to take off in the mid-50s was the monster movie. Nothing better demonstrated American paranoia about a Red menace than the sudden appearance of malevolent alien beings. Before independent studios began churning out microbudgeted flicks using stock music (such as Ed Wood's ultra-kitsch *Plan 9 From Outer Space* in 1958), there were plenty of innovative storylines and scores. No movie better demonstrated the genre than *Invasion Of The Body Snatchers* (1955). It presented its imaginative rendition of the McCarthy witch-hunts with subtlety and intelligence. A few similarly themed films preceded it like *The Thing From Another World* (1951), with an eerie score from Dimitri Tiomkin, *The Beast From 20,000 Fathoms* (1953), *Them!* and *Creature From The Black Lagoon* (both 1954), *Tarantula* and *It Came From Beneath The Sea* (both 1955). Aside from captivating titles and a general theme of constant attack from space, sea or atomic laboratories, these, and many others, shared a sense of adventure in their scoring when they weren't compiled from existing material. The names Herman Stein, Irving Gertz and Henry Mancini cropped up repeatedly in credits, and they were among several pioneers of experimental otherworldliness in film music. The theremin was an easy way of creating an unsettling atmosphere, and the trio's score for *It Came From Outer Space* (1953) is a terrific example. It was Universal Studios' first sci-fi invasion picture, and the composers were recruited to do more than merely jolt the audience at every 3-D effect. Their use of it was about as far as electronic enhancement could go at that point.

1956 was the watershed for non-orchestral scoring, when American couple Louis and Bebe Barron applied cybernetic technology to provide a completely electronic score for *Forbidden Planet*. It was called 'Electronic Tonalities' in the credits, but was for all intents and purposes a replacement of orchestral leitmotifs with sound-effect ones. Loveable Robby The Robot has his own, and so does the invisible id monster. The sounds came from unpredictable noise emissions from purpose-built experimental circuit boards. Although arguments abounded as to whether it truly constituted music, no one could deny there'd never been anything like it before. What made it a more important step was that anyone who wanted to develop the idea further had almost a full decade to wait before Robert Moog would produce the first synthesiser.

While Hollywood explored monsters of the future, the British Hammer studio revived interest in the supernatural terrors of the past. Specifically, they exhumed the characters Universal Studios had enjoyed success with 2 decades earlier. Following in the lumbering footsteps of Bela Lugosi and Boris Karloff came Christopher Lee, usually with Peter Cushing in hot pursuit. Hammer had been around in one form or another from the 30s, but their colour debut *The Quatermass Experiment* in 1954 made their name. John Hollingsworth was recruited as music supervisor for the studio, a role akin to those at the Hollywood music departments. He in turn launched the career of gentleman composer James Bernard, who stayed on board for an astonishing 25 years, providing dozens of scores and always seeming to get the best of the classic monsters and their very many sequels. That first *Quatermass* was followed by *X The Unknown* (1956) and the unimaginatively entitled sequel *Quatermass 2* (1957). These three scores are an amazing display of what we might now label modernism, with spare use of a small percussion and string ensemble. It was a sound that perfectly complemented the cold scientific paranoia on display in each film.

The Curse Of Frankenstein (1957) was a huge international success for Hammer, positioning the studio amongst the major players. For Bernard it was a moment of stylistic definition. His predilection for thematic title music created a melody line that's a singalong of the film's name. As the studio became known as Hammer Horror, he became the "Hammer Horror Composer". This was settled for good the following year with their adaptation of *Dracula*. Continuing the idea of musical notes as syllables of the title, his main theme is as identifiable a signature motif as any in cinema. Bernard carved his distinctive style into the minds of horror fans with a seemingly endless supply of dizzyingly fast string scherzos and tender love themes. Follow-ups to *Dracula* and *Frankenstein* continued into the 60s, during which time he also brought to life *The Gorgon* (1964), *She* (1965) with a trance-like ethereal theme, *The Plague Of The Zombies* (1966) and *The Devil Rides Out* (1968) with some genuinely unnerving backing for Satanic worship.

At Hammer's entry point in the mid-50s, it was quite a novelty for international films to be so happily changing hands across the ocean. British product occasionally found favour in America, but Hollywood studios still jealously guarded their territory. Those that did find distribution began to change that. RKO managed to pique curiosity about Japanese cinema by distributing Akira Kurosawa's *Rashomon* in 1952, with a gentle score by Fumio Hayasaka full of ethnic instrumentation that fascinated the Western ear. In many ways it was "The King Of The Monsters" who made enough noise for cult fandom to demand more international fare. *Godzilla* (1954) was inspired by *The Beast From 20,000 Fathoms* from the year before, but was unlike any monster seen before. The guy-in-a-suit approach made for a cheesy cinema experience, but you couldn't help but take a lot of it seriously due to the straight-faced music from Akira Ifukube. Later dubbed "The John Williams Of The Japanese Film World," his imperious 'Godzilla March' became the theme for the entire (long) series of films.

At the end of the decade, another example of cinematic immigration began filling US theatres with the beginnings of the French New Wave. In 1959, the release of François Truffaut's *Les Quatre Cents Coups* (*Four*

Hundred Blows) and Jean-Luc Godard's *A Bout De Souffle* (*Breathless*) turned eyes and ears toward Europe. Possessed of a casual, detached manner in their character observation, the genre sat perfectly alongside the rebellion of James Dean and rock 'n' roll.

It's important to note the beginnings of the genre here in the context of changes contributing to the birth of the Silver Age. We'll return to international film and the great director/composer relationships that formed and cemented in the 60s in Chapter 4. Now, courtesy of mentioning Truffaut, with whom Bernard Herrmann would scorch wonders for *Fahrenheit 451* (1966), we can turn to the most important collaboration in film music.

Silver Psycho

Alfred Hitchcock had worked with many composers throughout his career. We've covered lots of those names before Herrmann already, but it's worth stressing at this halfway point in the chronology of film music that these two men jointly influenced the industry far more than is generally realised. Their first collaboration was for *The Trouble With Harry* (1955), a jet black comedy about Shirley MacLaine and friends desperately trying to dispose of a corpse. For his one and only comedic score, Herrmann had fun mimicking the pratfalls and macabre shenanigans. The sense of humour fits both their personalities perfectly, cementing their relationship. Hitchcock was unable to think of working with another composer for the next decade. They totted up another seven films in their 11 years together.

Next came a remake of the director's own work with *The Man Who Knew Too Much* (1956), with James Stewart and Doris Day embroiled in the world of kidnapping and espionage. Although Herrmann wrote a comparatively short score, he was given one of the most prominent on-screen cameos any film composer has had. During an assassination attempt at The Royal Albert Hall, the camera lingers on a poster advertising his name, before cutting to show him authoritatively conducting the London Symphony Orchestra. His appearance is a visual cue for the film's finale to begin and the stage/screen music becomes narrator for the action instead of dialogue. It was a strong indication that Hitchcock appreciated and acknowledged the contribution of Herrmann's music. Use of the song 'Que Sera, Sera' was an indication that even the great director was subject to the beginnings of studio pressure to plug commercial songs. The same year they released *The Wrong Man*, with Henry Fonda reliving a true story of mistaken identity. Taking the character's job as a jazz bassist to begin with, the score is cold and claustrophobic, managing to infer the confines of imprisonment. Although the film may be overshadowed by what followed, it has many scenes illustrating the way music can pre-empt danger and tell an audience what a character is thinking.

With *Vertigo* (1958), the director and composer made use of many similar tricks, and even invented some new ones. It's the most personal film for them both. Themes of obsession and death were appealing, and found romantic expression in what is regarded as one of the greatest motion pictures of all time (despite being mildly maligned in its day). Scottie Ferguson's phobia, loneliness and infatuation are explained to us almost exclusively through music since there are long sequences without dialogue. At the climax of the thrilling rooftop chase that opens the film, the first display of James Stewart's vertigo is illustrated with overlapping harp glissandos (rapid sliding up and down scales). In the extended sequence trailing Madeleine (Kim Novak) around San Francisco, it's entirely down to the music that we're drawn into the mystery of what's happening instead of being bored by a silent car tour of the city. The art gallery scene is a brilliant showcase of Herrmann manipulating our understanding of what's going on. The portrait of Carlotta bears physical resemblance to Madeleine, so is she supernaturally possessed or just insane? The score provides both answers simultaneously. The most famous cue from the score, entitled 'Scène d'Amour,' has inspired countless references and spoofs, such as a great visual gag incorporated into *Twelve Monkeys* (1995). Novak reappears as Judy, and then magically transforms back into Madeleine. The magic is evoked as much through surreal colour saturation and imagery as by one of Herrmann's most heartfelt compositions capturing the very essence of yearning and desire.

Paramount Studios didn't succeed in persuading Hitchcock to make use of a song for *Vertigo* thankfully. Although he wanted to sustain that principle for *North By Northwest* (1959), the interlude music (a reprise of the love theme) became a reasonably popular tune. It was certainly a better idea than a song called 'The Man On Lincoln's Nose.' The film is constantly on the move, either literally or by plot twists carrying audiences dizzyingly along. What Herrmann did for the chase movie was have fun with it. The fandango of the main titles is an unpredictable piece built on rhythms that swirl around one another without resolution, and are the foundation to a motif equally elusive and tongue-in-cheek. There are two scenes within the film performing opposite functions to one another. Scrabbling over the face of Mount Rushmore for the finale, the action continues without dialogue for some time. It's left to the score to make this interesting (in the same way as Scottie's pursuit of Maddy in *Vertigo*), and this is where the title's fandango pays off as a musical device. Hand-in-hand, Roger Thornhill (Cary Grant) and Eve Kendall (Eva Marie Saint) skip and climb the rock face, and the editing maintains a rhythm to which the furious dance is perfectly suited. The other infamous scene is of Grant being chased down by a flying crop duster, which is devoid of music. Director and composer agreed a heightened reality was achieved by allowing natural sound effects to guide the ear. Only when the plane crashes does the music strike up. Knowing when to stop the music later led to their big experiment in using none at all for *The Birds* (1963).

So we come to *Psycho* (1960), a film that perhaps more than any other shows how film music can live outside the film itself. Regardless of whether they've seen the film or not, kids of all ages know what sound to make when they tease about stabbing one another. TV adverts, movie spoofs and homages have kept the shower-murder music alive in popular culture. What a lot of people don't know is that Hitchcock didn't want music for the scene, and that Herrmann wrote and recorded the piece in secret. When the director made the choice to shoot in black and white (despite studios by then insisting on colour to make subsidiary sales to television easier), Herrmann made an intellectual leap to composing a black and white score by restricting himself to using only the string section of an orchestra. For the murder, which required what he adroitly called "terror," the shrieking effect came from part of a violinist's tuning-up routine. So simple a device has become the most mimicked musical effect in cinema history. The rest of the score works to the picture's benefit just as well. Herrmann's unnervingly chaotic opening title music actually inspired the animation from Saul Bass. Much more importantly, the script left long sequences without dialogue and once again director/composer intended music to act as emotional and psychological narrator. Marion's anxious drive having stolen some money is a sequence often cited by musicologists for this technique. Switch off the volume, and the shots of Janet Leigh at the wheel could be taking her anywhere. Turn the volume back up, and the urgent score makes it quite clear that the movie title is going to pay off very soon.

The film was remade in 1997 by Gus Van Sant, and that allowed for a brand new digital recording of the score. It was affectionately adapted to the new version by Herrmann's biggest fan, Danny Elfman.

There are several factors to blame for the eventual split between Herrmann and Hitchcock, and unfortunately music had a lot to do with it. After the experiment of *The Birds*, and the all-round failure of *Marnie* (1964), everything came to a head with *Torn Curtain* (1966). The studios had been nibbling away at Hitch to get him in line and sticking commercial songs somewhere in his films. On top of that, he'd gone from being respectfully grateful of the extent to which Herrmann's music improved his work, to being downright resentful. It all exploded at the *Torn Curtain* recording sessions when the music turned out not to be the requested pop style. Everyone thought they were individually right, and for such a mediocre movie it's a shame none of them were.

Through this transitional Silver Age period, Herrmann had contributed to the very start of the alien-invasion genre with one of its best films and scores, *The Day The Earth Stood Still* (1951). He'd also contributed to the religious epic genre with *The Egyptian* (1954), splitting cues between himself and music department chief Alfred Newman. It proved to be his most prolific period, and was rounded out by boisterous fun for a brief flirtation with the fantasy genre. *The Seventh Voyage Of Sinbad* (1958), *Journey To The Centre Of The Earth* (1959), *The Three Worlds Of Gulliver* (1960), *Mysterious Island* (1961) and *Jason And The Argonauts* (1963) musically defined one monster or another, such as the xylophone for the skeleton warriors in *The Seventh Voyage Of Sinbad*.

When you add together rock 'n' roll, new technologies in sight and sound, the influence of international musical styles, flavour-of-the-month exploitation genres, the start and end of Hitchcock and Herrmann, and the fact that 1955 was the year videotape was introduced, what you get is a period of changing styles that's clearly different from the more self-contained sound of the Golden Age. As the Silver Age entered the 60s, a lot of what composers like Herrmann had to offer was pushed out. The seeds had been sown, largely out of financial necessity, and now the studios wanted as commercial a product as possible.

4. Commercial Instincts

One of the better things to come from the 50s' technological advancement was bringing international film into greater focus outside its country of origin. The French New Wave is a good example because of its trendsetting and rebellious nature towards social and film-making attitudes. During the 60s, whenever Hollywood couldn't encourage the new musical sounds it heard from overseas into its own films, it encouraged the composers to cross over themselves. Georges Delerue was an émigré from France. After a couple of years work, his career was launched and secured with *Shoot The Piano Player* (1960) for director François Truffaut. It began a ten-picture collaboration. Their second, *Jules And Jim* (1961), has remained the most admired and well known with its collision of carefree meets catastrophe. Delerue's upbeat carnivalesque 'Main Title' would go on to help define the comedic writing style both in its own decade, and later again in the 80s (see Danny Elfman, Chapter 6). Their relationship continued with *Love At 20: Antoine And Colette* (1962), *The Soft Skin* (1964), *Such A Gorgeous Kid Like Me* (1971), *Two English Girls* (1971) and their other most affectionately revered piece, *Day For Night* (1973), with its stunning chorale (hymn-like tune) for an aerial view montage of the set for fictional film 'Meet Pamela.'

Another French success that played the film-within-a-film idea was director Jean-Luc Godard's *Contempt* (1963). Delerue provided stormy emotional turmoil for strings as we watch the dissolution of a marriage on set. Just before Hollywood enticed Delerue away, the decade also heard some delightful period English music for the historical tales *A Man For All Seasons* (1966) and *Anne Of The Thousand Days* (1969). Through all these works, he displayed not just an ear for instrumentation and locale, but that he was one of the finest melody writers film music ever knew. He was asked to recreate this sound repeatedly in the 70s and 80s on American pictures like Oliver Stone's *Salvador* and *Platoon* (both 1986), and *Steel Magnolias*, *Beaches* and *Biloxi Blues* (all 1988).

The charming antics of French comic genius Jacques Tati predated Delerue. *Monsieur Hulot's Holiday* found an international audience in 1953 and it helped associate the use of piano, accordion and guitar with the French. This was courtesy of composer Alain Romans who went on to co-score Tati's *My Uncle* (1958) with Franck Barcellini. A decade later, Francis Lemarque reminded the industry of the comedy stereotype with *Playtime* (1967). A manic waltz and furious Can-Can led by fairground

organ grace the finale where the traffic of central Paris is choreographed as a carnival funfair.

The Cannes Film Festival became the place to make foreign territory discoveries. It took about 20 years for Hollywood to pay serious attention to the event, but when *A Man And A Woman* won the Palme d'Or in 1966 it changed the careers of director Claude Lelouch and composer Francis Lai. Clearly something in the combination of "da-ba-da-ba-da" lyrics and accordion fell right into place with the new wave of pop music listeners because the score album was in the US charts for 93 weeks! Lelouch and Lai carved out a lasting working relationship, with *Live For Life* (1967), *And Now My Love* (1974), *Bolero* (1981) and two sequels to *A Man And A Woman*. Lai was another to end up working on American films, with his biggest success being *Love Story* (1970), which spawned several versions of its song 'Where Do I Begin?' and won him his only Academy Award.

Eclipsing the awards in Hollywood and France, the chart successes, the length of tenure with a director and popularity with public and critics alike is Nino Rota. The Italian composer began working with Federico Fellini in 1952 on *The White Sheik*. They did sixteen films together of which at least six are considered masterpieces of cinema and its music. The brightest jewel is *La Dolce Vita* (1960), which follows a journalist observing Rome high life. Rota offers an enormous musical range for scenes of a bustling metropolis contrasting with decadence behind closed doors. The jazz/pop fusion found immediate favour with the social type it portrayed and the audience who aspired to that lifestyle. Next came *8½* (1963), autobiographically depositing the life of a film director into an unpredictable dreamworld. Of all the composer's circus-styled marches, those here have remained the most admired and influential. Along with Delerue's *Jules And Jim*, it would contribute much to the comedies of the mid-80s. Going on to the variable successes of *Juliet Of The Spirits* (1965), *Satyricon* (1969), *The Clowns* (1970), *Roma* (1972), *Amarcord* (1973) and *Casanova* (1976), the composer and director shared nearly 30 years of screen time.

Nino Rota's work in Europe continued elsewhere too of course. For director Luchino Visconti he provided grand historical portraits for *Rocco And His Brothers* (1960) and *The Leopard* (1963). For Sergei Bondarchuk there were waltzes on and off the battlefield in depicting Napoleon's *Waterloo* (1970). For Franco Zeffirelli, two Shakespearean adaptations led to him inevitably being whisked away to the States. *The Taming Of The Shrew* (1967) was a spirited comedic turn to his gift for melody, but with *Romeo And Juliet* (1968) the ability to conjure time and place (here mock-medieval) found its finest voice with what may well be the definitive romantic love theme. The album spent 74 weeks in US charts. A 'Love Theme' single was a Number 1 hit as adapted by Henry Mancini. It has also seen many spoofs in film, as well as found many new homes in advertising and media (e.g. endless play on UK radio). Director Francis Ford Coppola was much enamoured with the piece and, bolstered with their shared Italian heritage, made Rota the perfect choice for *The Godfather* (1972). It lost out on an Academy Award because the theme had been used before in another guise on an earlier score. Developing the infamous Mafia family's themes for the sequel, *The Godfather Part II* (1974), he won an Oscar then instead, which is a unique achievement in sequel scoring. Then, in the year before his untimely death, he gave American film the infectiously memorable theme for an Egyptian paddle steamer carrying the weight of a *Death On The Nile* (1978).

Riding The Sixties Side-Saddle

The Western was one of cinema's original genres and has only truly disappeared from screens over the last few decades. As Tiomkin's output showed, especially with *High Noon*, audiences still loved the pretence of Cowboys and Indians as the 50s became the 60s. Composer Jerome Moross scored less than twenty films, and mainly worked behind the scenes as an orchestrator. An association with Aaron Copland led to him creating his own brand of Americana which is nowhere better illustrated than in *The Big Country* (1958). The rolling melody of its main theme is as perfect a description of the open skies and sprawling deserts of the Old West as the film title itself. The same year he also produced *The Proud Rebel*, then *The Jayhawkers!* (1959) and the theme to TV's *Wagon Train*. His *Big Country* music was to be the defining work of his film and concert hall career though. In a public popularity contest for the most memorable Western theme there are only two other contenders. Elmer Bernstein's hero theme for *The Magnificent Seven* (1960) became an instant template for anyone wanting to musically conjure noble team spirit. With hindsight, its reuse for a long-running series of Marlboro cigarette ads wasn't all that flattering! The other immortal Western theme belongs to *How The West Was Won* (1962) by Alfred Newman. There's an unparalleled optimism in the piece that cannot help but make the listener smile. Years later, it's all-round good cheer pleased director Robert

Zemeckis so much that despite *Romancing The Stone* (1984) being his first collaboration with composer Alan Silvestri, he would settle for nothing else to open the movie on.

The other Italian composer to make his international mark during the 60s was Ennio Morricone. His work for director Sergio Leone was instantly declared to be its own genre. Their *Dollars* trilogy turned many conventions on their heads, and remains wholly individual from some four hundred movies that tried to copy them. Hollywood dubbed them Spaghetti Westerns, which is a bit lacking as a description. Starting with *A Fistful Of Dollars* (1964), the films were designed to dazzle in visual prowess, with Morricone creating music to act as an additional character. Our introduction to Clint Eastwood as the Man With No Name is via solo whistler, whip cracks, bells, animalistic choral grunts and electric guitar. This combination of layered elements is so abstract from the visuals you have to pay attention to it.

Since the experiment worked, it was taken further for the sequels. *For A Few Dollars More* (1965) keeps the whistler, adds the twanging of a Jew's Harp (a strip of steel you bite and strum), then fires up snare drums to mimic horseback riders at full gallop. One extraordinary set piece for the cue 'Paying Off Scores' has a music box tinkle, unprecedented levels of hard guitar twanging, castanets, Mexican horns and surreal burst of church organ. The quirky orchestrations go further still for *The Good, The Bad And The Ugly* (1966) which has always been the real cult classic. Here some of the elements seem to fuse and talk to one another. The whistles work in tandem and the crazed coyote-howl motif is answered by what seems like a sucker-punch reply of "wah wah-wah." It all builds up to a balletic finale when the gold-seeking trio square off at a graveyard and the music takes over completely.

One more collaboration from the 60s remains a cult film thanks to Morricone loading natural sound and obscure stylistic collisions with ominous meaning. *Once Upon A Time In The West* (1969) is a fond farewell to the Cowboy's West. The ghostly female soprano voice given to illustrate this impending loss is one of the most emotional responses to a film's overall theme a composer ever made. There's also the most prominent example of his method of growing something organically from the fabric of the movie. Charles Bronson's shocking revenge motive isn't revealed until the very end. Once seen, repeat viewing make every note of his 'Harmonica Theme' all the more chilling.

Morricone's daring juxtaposition of sounds and layers of rhythm had a wide effect on contemporary music. Recording technology wasn't available to do what's possible today, but by looping the layered elements he was for all intents and purposes applying the principles of sampling. In later decades, it is rare to find these principles in his work. Instead he has become more appreciated for the romantic highs of *The Mission* (1986) and *Cinema Paradiso* (1989) or the action/thriller suspense of *The Untouchables* (1987) and *In The Line Of Fire* (1993).

A couple of additional internationally influential composers deserve mention here. First is Mikis Theodorakis from Greece, whose political activities led to a period in prison and a ban on his music before release and exile. During this period he nonetheless produced highly memorable works for *Elektra* (1962), *Phaedra* (1962), *Zorba The Greek* (1964) and *Z* (1969). The last of these won several Oscars, but ignored the exciting score for bouzouki and orchestra. Of real influence to chart music was *Black Orpheus* in 1959. Brazilian composer Luiz Bonfa, together with Antonio Carlos Jobim, introduced jazz samba to a worldwide audience, and in so doing made the bossa nova a musical trademark for the next decade.

Making The Sixties Swing

With the youth market caught up in a world of music they'd embraced as their own, Hollywood was keen to pursue every financial avenue open to them. Giving pop stars their own movies was one way of drawing audiences in and getting subsidiary record sales. Elvis Presley had been the biggest proof that this worked with successful albums from *GI Blues* (1960), *Blue Hawaii* (1961), *Girls! Girls! Girls!* (1962), *Fun In Acapulco* (1963) and *Roustabout* (1964). Then The Beatles did the same thing for both the UK and America with *A Hard Day's Night* (1964), *Help!* (1965) and *Yellow Submarine* (1969). The only problem the studios had with encouraging more of these was the spiralling costs of the stars and their music. Inevitably, they turned to film composers to pull a rabbit from the hat as often as possible with a hit song or two of their own. Fortunately there were several new talents more than up to the challenge.

A way of killing two birds with one stone was to poach composers from the realms of television. By 1965 it posed another threat with the advent of continuous colour and international transmissions. An easy target was the author of the *Peter Gunn* series theme which had a Grammy-winning LP. Henry Mancini subsequently became one of the most important names in music during the 60s. This sparse economy of orchestration in *Peter Gunn* meant he was encouraged to differ noticeably from the Golden Age sound. His hip, swinging, Hammond organ and flute combo is a quintessentially defining sound for the decade. He won his first pair of Oscars with *Breakfast At Tiffany's* in 1961. The enormous popularity of the song 'Moon River' ensured that for almost every subsequent picture he scored, the studios expected another hit. Through his prolific association with director Blake Edwards (you'll be gathering by now that these relationships are rather important), Mancini managed to keep studios regularly happy. *The Pink Panther* (1963) is ample proof. Its saxophone tune is one of the most celebrated motifs in film music history. As an album it spent 88 weeks in US charts, and has appeared on countless compilations from the period. Seven sequel films followed, all still with Edwards. His other double Oscar win came with *Hatari!* (1962) for director Howard Hawks. The song 'Baby Elephant Walk' was a boogie-woogie sensation despite the film's fairly serious tone for an African safari. Mancini was a great proponent of his belief that music should be heard in film. It contradicted a lot of what composers who came before believed, but it's one of the things that singles him out as at the forefront of a new way of thinking about the industry. He deplored the fact that jazz was applied inappropriately in film and TV after his *Peter Gunn* stint, and liked it even less when the studios tried to squeeze every drop of commerciality out of pop music applied to film.

As a result of these feelings, his post-60s career diversified far more into other genres. Prior to the decade of swing, he'd worked on a lot of monster pictures and the odd excursion into dark psychological territory (e.g. *Touch Of Evil* in 1958). All too suddenly the comedic label he'd become stuck with proved hard to shake. Especially when more serious 70s fare failed at the box office. He'd always had a terrific sense of drama and imagination for instrumentation, but applying it to *The Molly Maguires* (1970) or *Silver Streak* (1976) did him little favours. A lot of his work in the 70s therefore returned him to his roots in TV, providing themes.

The next name lifted from 60s TV credits was Lalo Schifrin whose jazz-laced work showed his gift for rhythm and percussion. Coming from a classical and jazz background in his native Buenos Aires, he was the perfect choice to apply both to the Steve McQueen poker movie *The Cincinnati Kid* (1965). Industry ears really pricked up the following year with his TV theme to *Mission: Impossible*. It's as well known today as then by virtue of its often-mimicked beat, and also two recent big-budget features - Danny Elfman adapted the theme in 1996 and Hans Zimmer in

2000. It was his ability to effortlessly create authentic sounding geographical backgrounds in combination with any number of musical styles that made him highly sought after. In 1967 he put southern bluegrass beneath the feet of Paul Newman as *Cool Hand Luke*. Then with a minute ensemble of ten instruments he implied sexual tension between two ladies' lives interrupted by *The Fox* in 1968. That year also saw the release of the second of Schifrin's cult successes (again with McQueen) for *Bullitt*. It has become the most well known use of jazz in film because of a car commercial in the late 90s, which prompted a premiere CD release of the score and chart single. Its laid-back cool for big band jazz ensemble, dramatic counterpoint, and handful of radio source pieces (the term for music playing somewhere within a film) is a brilliant example of scoring a film from every intellectual angle.

The third of the high-profile projects that Schifrin is famous for is the *Dirty Harry* series, for which he scored four out of the five starting in 1971. Electric piano gave Harry Callahan a tough edge to match Clint Eastwood's sneer, and wordless female voices echoed the madness raging inside serial killer Scorpio's head. Both made for an eerie atmosphere keeping the outcome of the film open all the way through. The jazz/rock element made it very contemporary to the 60s (and fashionable again today), and alongside *Bullitt* the music makes San Francisco seem like the most happening place on Earth!

Bruce Lee's explosive introduction to mainstream Western audiences was *Enter The Dragon* (1973). Schifrin used traditional Chinese scales alongside his trademark funky backbeats to keep things authentic yet purposefully tongue-in-cheek, as Lee dispatches whole armies of goons. Contrasting style, but not his preference for research, was *The Four Musketeers* (1974). The air of high adventure via late-Renaissance period music showed that Golden Age thinking still had its place. That said, he did also compose the *Planet Of The Apes* and *Starsky And Hutch* TV themes the same year...

Making The Sixties Sing

With financial considerations foremost on their minds, the studios really loved anyone who could overlap with the pop music scene. From this perspective, the indisputable king of songwriting through the 60s was Burt Bacharach. His work as musical director for Marlene Dietrich led to teaming with lyricist Hal David. Together they'd already penned innumerable classic tunes when Hollywood gave them *What's New, Pussy-cat!* and *After The Fox* to play with in 1965. *What's New, Pussycat?* has a waltz-like underscore, which throws a kazoo into its unpredictable mix. The title song was cleverly given to Tom Jones, who'd only just hit the big time with 'It's Not Unusual.' A Dionne Warwick track ('Here I Am') secured Bacharach's working relationship with her for many years. *After The Fox* was less of a song-oriented film, with only The Hollies' title tune to back the upbeat yet melodic underscore.

Bacharach's next demonstration of what made the 60s swing was the James Bond spoof *Casino Royale* (1967). With David Niven, Woody Allen and Peter Sellers playing it all for laughs, the music is at times made almost surreal in atmosphere by Mickey-Mousing the madcap antics. Due to the film's box-office misfire, its title track remained an instrumental instead of being adapted with lyrics. 'The Look Of Love' sung in husky sensual fashion by Dusty Springfield has remained one of the composer's many well-known tunes nonetheless. Far outweighing these others (and all that followed) was 'Raindrops Keep Fallin' On My Head' from *Butch Cassidy And The Sundance Kid* (1969). It was a Number 1 hit and, in conjunction with his jaunty original score, helped Bacharach to win two Oscars. At the time, the use of contemporary method scoring and tracking a scene by song was seen as inappropriate in some quarters for a movie about 19th-Century cowboy bandits. It was exactly the sort of thing Mancini had observed occurring in film scoring, and knew it would only take a few moneymakers to start making the traditional film composer's role look out of place. As recognition for Bacharach's contribution to the sound of the 60s, could there be any higher praise than his cameos in both *Austin Powers* movies with spoof scores from George S Clinton?

There were three other significant contributions to the philosophy adopted by major studios during the decade. First, the score for *The Graduate* (1967) was designed by acquiring the license to reuse existing pop songs. This meant lyrics and rhythms had nothing to do with the film. Instead they were chosen for the tone of a scene and as a part of what was hoped would be a best-selling album. Director Mike Nichols is credited with the idea. The fact that the album, its one original song ('Mrs Robinson'), and Simon And Garfunkel's next album (*Bookends*) all went straight to Number 1 seems to indicate that some part of that idea was spot on.

Dave Grusin provided an original score for *The Graduate*, but nobody remembers that. The same thing happened to Michel Legrand's score for

The Thomas Crown Affair (1968). 'The Windmills Of Your Mind' eclipsed not only the fine jazz/classic-influenced score, but also most of Legrand's career outside his native France.

Taking things one step further was *Easy Rider* (1969), which cobbled together its soundtrack from actor/director Dennis Hopper's record collection. It was one of the year's biggest movies. Producers were convinced this was the way to go to encourage the disposable income youth group into cinemas with their favourite songs. A slew of similar philosophically disenchanted films followed, all with song playlists made up of chart successes from recent years. This philosophy has continued to the present day, which is a bone of contention in a collectors' market overrun with CDs that have nothing to do with the films they promote.

Shaking And Stirring The Sixties

The decade also continued the Silver Age's combination of musical styles and experimentation by composers whose commercial instincts were secondary to the dramatic purpose by which they served a film.

"My approach to scoring a film is to look at the whole thing at once," reveals John Barry. "I identify an overall message or emotion and score that. I always go for a melody first, because it's the most direct form of communication dramatically. It has to be versatile though. It's one theme being used in many different ways. Shostakovich said about music keeping the emotion intact. Once you capture that essence everything else springs from that daddy, that master file. You grow with other harmonic material. Maybe take fractions of the melody. That starts to dictate the rest of the score for you. I do love having a theme that works throughout, although it's not possible on every single film of course." This insight from the British composer defines a 40-year career in film scoring. A combination of happy coincidences took Barry from his jazzy beat band The John Barry Seven to *Beat Girl* (1960). His ear for arrangement of material and finger-on-the-pulse of popular style was exactly what studios wanted. In 1962, the production team overseeing the adaptation of Ian Fleming's James Bond character to the big screen were very keen to apply some of Barry's commercial style.

For 40 years there's been a contentious issue about ownership of the 'James Bond Theme.' All the individual movie albums and countless Bond compilations on shelves credit Monty Norman, who scored the whole of Sean Connery's debut in the role for *Dr No* (1962). Barry was asked to work his arranging wizardry on material that didn't suit producers' ears. A March 2001 court case determined Norman was unfairly discredited in a newspaper article that implicitly identified Barry as the sole writer. Rather predictably, the libel case was mistaken by the press for a decision of ownership. Suffice to say, the fan community debate continues. In many ways, the issue is rather immaterial since it was Barry who went on to score the bulk of the rest the series. *From Russia With Love* followed in 1963. Although it introduced his '007 Theme' and his idea of an overall theme being used within a credit sequence song, its success was completely outdone by *Goldfinger* the following year. Shirley Bassey's knockout vocals for the title song contributed to making it a Number 1 hit album staying in US charts far longer than in the UK. This second instalment clearly established that as well as his melodic sense and knack for jazzy arranging, Barry was also capable of rhythmically charged action music. Altogether it formed a template for anyone wanting a hit film song, or to score one of the numerous spy movie wannabes that soon appeared.

Through *Thunderball* (1965), *You Only Live Twice* (1967) and *On Her Majesty's Secret Service* (1969), his style developed to the point of forming its own genre. With *Diamonds Are Forever* (1971) there was a subtle gear shift in tone to reflect changing attitudes, making the music more commercial than ever. The film's score acknowledged that pop was ready to go disco in a few years time, and early 70s funk was the stylistic transition. Some of the lyrics penned by regular collaborator Don Black caused Barry minor controversy ("touch it, stroke it and undress it"). Even if the song wasn't as big a hit as *Goldfinger*, it's still one of the most well known of the Bond songs and of Shirley Bassey's repertoire. Barry subsequently skipped *Live And Let Die* (1973) where the funk was laid on in spades by George Martin and Paul McCartney's song. The Bond series has always been inextricably linked with Barry's name regardless of other composers' entries though. This isn't all there was from Barry in the decade however.

An on-screen association with Michael Caine began in 1964 with *Zulu*. This score shows Barry's economy with material to great effect in only 16 minutes of original music. Its central theme does a two-for-one job of depicting the bravery of both the British infantry and the native warriors. It was the first opportunity for Barry to properly flex his dramatic muscles, since he considered the Bond movies to be essentially cartoon-like. Then his jazz roots shone through the score for youth culture sensation *The Knack... And How To Get It* (1965) with a heavy leaning on organ, which was a hugely popular instrument at the time. For *The Ipcress File* (1965), he showed off a Hungarian instrument almost no one knew of (the cimbalom) for the memorable 'A Man Alone' theme characterising anti-hero Harry Palmer (Caine again).

His first two Oscars came side-by-side in 1967 for the true story of Elsa the lion cub in *Born Free* (1966). Both score and song (lyrics again by Don Black) were awarded and became enormous worldwide hits as an album and single. In fact, the song was covered by more than six hundred artists in a matter of months after initial release, and even wound up as national anthem for one African state. Here at the very height of his popularity, Barry composed what remains a personal favourite to the present day: *The Lion In Winter* (1968). It illustrated how the 12th-Century English royalty clashed with the Church of Rome. Unusually for Barry, he used a chorus and wrote two period-specific songs. He won another Academy Award for the score.

That same year, like Herrmann in *The Man Who Knew Too Much*, Barry conducted a concerto on screen for the finale of *Deadfall*. Barry wrote his piece however, and it was a mark of industry trust he did so in advance of the film being shot, which was then edited to the music. There was another song for Shirley Bassey ('My Love Has Two Faces'), but regrettably the film failed to live up to its promise and so his 'Romance For Guitar And Orchestra' has remained unheard beyond the soundtrack. Rounding out the decade was another of his favourites, *Midnight Cowboy* (1969). As a conceptualised project it was a product of the commercially oriented times. However, it's a very different beast from the song-tracked films mentioned already. "It's still shown at UCLA Film School as the best example of song in film," says the composer with understandable pride. "We didn't go out and just buy a bunch of songs. It was all written especially for the scenes. It was literally a case of scoring with songs, and I took a lot of care with it. The scene where he steals bread and is spotted and shamed just kills you. The loneliness of that song ('Old Man Willow' by Elephant's Memory) drifting down over it had an atmosphere I couldn't have got with a score. If it's done right it can be terribly effective." Sadly it seldom is done right, but Barry has avoided accusation of being one to do it wrong by never working on a film in the same way again. Although the Bond pictures continued, each requiring an acknowledgement of the pop style of the day in their title song, he gradually became drawn to more romantically themed projects. Escaping the typecasting of being a teen/spy/pop culture composer, Barry's music of the

80s and 90s is distinguished for its blend of flowing melody, cleverly wrought counterpoint (secondary melody) and tender expressiveness.

At War In The Sixties

Although the decade's real-life war was the Vietnam conflict, it was World War Two that Hollywood repeatedly put on the big screen. There had been newsreel propaganda exercises aplenty during the period of the battle. A few respectful adventure tales appeared in the 50s too, such as *The Bridge On The River Kwai* (1957), with Sir Malcolm Arnold's Oscar-winning score famously using the whistle-along 'Colonel Bogey March.' No one thought to glorify the American perspective until the 60s. Since only so much historical accuracy can be shoehorned into 120 minutes, it would often fall by the wayside. The most successful template to follow became having a stellar cast of crack troops sent on some do-or-die mission. For composers, the mission was to characterise the Nazis in suitably villainous fashion and the Allies as contemporary Round Table Knights of honour. Scores to typify the genre's sudden popularity included *Sink The Bismark!* (1960) from Clifton Parker, the Greek-tinged anthems for Gregory Peck defeating the whole German army in *The Guns Of Navarone* (1962) from Dimitri Tiomkin, *Battle Of The Bulge* (1965) from Benjamin Frankel, *Attack On The Iron Coast* (1967) from Gerard Schurmann and the other whistle-along camaraderie-in-crisis anthem of *The Great Escape* (1963) from Elmer Bernstein.

If there's one musical constant in war movies, it's that the military moves to a beat. It's therefore not surprising that the composer who came to score more WWII flicks than anyone else in the decade was a percussionist at heart. Maurice Jarre (father of Jean-Michel) was an international discovery who benefited from the Silver Age's open door policy to ideas. After a decade of local fare, the French composer's first explosive battle accompaniment was for *The Longest Day* (1962). That extremely noisy account of the Normandy landings was followed by *Weekend At Dunkirk* (1964), then *The Train* and *Is Paris Burning?* (both 1965). A waltzing tone poem for the latter honoured the liberation of the French capital. Two years on he scored a reasonably forgettable piece for *The Twenty-Fifth Hour* before crafting one of his most celebrated works for *The Night Of The Generals*. With sinister marches and a bouncing waltz, Jarre conjured distinct unease over which of several Nazi generals might be the murderer of a prostitute. Capping his contribution to the 60s cinematic war effort was *The Damned* (1969), an unsettling portrait of a family falling apart under Nazi influence. All these scores showed off his percussive skills and his pioneering of ethnic instrumentation, which audiences would be reminded of when he returned to the war a decade later for *The Tin Drum* (1979).

Although this arsenal of bombast kept his profile high, it had initially been fired into the stratosphere when he worked with director David Lean. The leading names of the day had been linked at one time or another to the epic *Lawrence Of Arabia* (1962), such as Malcolm Arnold, Benjamin Britten, Aram Khachaturian, Richard Rodgers and William Walton. Lean's ear was intrigued by Jarre's exotic score for *Sundays And Cybele* (1962), so Jarre was hired. What came out was another of cinema's great identifying motifs. The enduring desert theme won him his first Oscar and considerable recording industry clout with a soundtrack album remaining in US charts for 86 weeks. Remarkably, the director and composer managed to top the achievement with *Doctor Zhivago* a year later. If the *Lawrence Of Arabia* theme is the perfect desert music in the way that *Psycho* is the perfect murder music, or *Jaws* the perfect shark music, then 'Lara's Theme' from *Zhivago* must be the perfect romance music. It won him another Oscar and spent over 3 years in the charts! Lean and Jarre later reunited for *Ryan's Daughter* (1969) and *A Passage To India* (1984).

Back at the front line, when it came to the British perspective on the Second World War, Ron Goodwin was the composer who defined stiff upper lip better than anyone else. His music for *633 Squadron* (1964) is a perfect encapsulation of aerial militaria. For the soaring and swooping of a German munitions factory air raid, he used French horns to literally play the title (in 6-8 time, the theme is six short notes followed by three long ones). The following year he scored the aerial comedy *Those Magnificent Men In Their Flying Machines* as if it were an action movie, and cemented a style that has been paid homage to ever since. Hollywood was never averse to bending historical rules by way of best-selling authors who'd done so first. Alistair MacLean's leaning toward espionage and paranoia suited big-screen adaptation tremendously. With *Where Eagles Dare* (1969), Goodwin produced a fabulously memorable tension theme for Richard Burton's raid on a mountaintop Nazi castle. Then he went back into the air for a replacement score (more about which in Chapter 6) on *The Battle Of Britain* (1969), where his mimicking rat-a-tat effect served the Royal Air Force superbly.

Genre Gold (And Silver)

The legacy of Silver Age freedom, which originated in the 50s, was that new composers of the 60s (and onwards) were free to skip, create and define whole genres of film and music. If any one composer can lay claim to being a master of all genres, it is Jerry Goldsmith. In 40 years, he has had a musical hand in just about every conceivable type of film there is. Progressing from years working in television (writing the themes for *The Man From U.N.C.L.E.* and *Dr Kildare* amongst many others), it was in the 60s that his film career demonstrated it was possible to be a Jack of all trades. There were Westerns of varying quality, like *Rio Conchos* (1964), *Stagecoach* (1966), *Hour Of The Gun* (1967), *Bandolero!* (1968) and *100 Rifles* (1969). All feature a development of his powerhouse action writing combined with folksy homeliness. Later with *Take A Hard Ride* (1975) some clear references to the Spaghetti Western licks of Ennio Morricone were apparent. About the only other time he was obviously asked to emulate another style was for the Bond wannabes with James Coburn as *Our Man Flint* (1965). Both this and its sequel *In Like Flint* (1967) feature winks and tips of the hat with electric guitar and keyboards.

He was drawn to projects of a serious nature though, frequently leading to good critical notice. When you're dealing with racial issues for *A Patch Of Blue* (1965) or the turbulent 1920s politics of America and China for *The Sand Pebbles* (1966), subtlety is key. A small ensemble of musicians plays on each instead of full orchestra, and for *The Sand Pebbles* the Oriental colours and memorable love theme led to the popular song 'And We Were Lovers.' Throughout the 60s he was another of the composers who found themselves repeatedly immersed in WWII. The only exception being his bombastic yet balletic accompaniment for the aerial dogfights of *The Blue Max* (1966), which was a rare glimpse of WWI for the decade. He propelled the escape from an Italian POW camp aboard the *Von Ryan's Express* (1965). The same year he amusingly worked on the aftermath of the attack on Pearl Harbour before later scoring the event itself. *In Harm's Way* (1965) dealt with the US Navy's retaliation, and then *Tora! Tora! Tora!* (1970) showed an unbiased account of how they'd let it happen. In the second score, Goldsmith worked in as much Japanese patriotism (via appropriate Asian instrumentation) as he did American flag waving. It was one of many early indications he was at ease with all areas of music and not afraid to be geographically specific.

Goldsmith's most famous war drama score is *Patton* (1970). His ability with pared-down instrumentation is at its best in this account of the legendary general. Deciding on a mere 30 minutes of music in the course of 3 hours, he split the material between three aspects of the character: the religious (signified by organ), the military (a strong but sprightly march) and the spiritual (trumpets that echo away into silence). The last aspect was achieved with an echoplex, a device very much in vogue in the pop music world at the time. Its intellectual intent was to reflect Patton's belief in reincarnation. Over the years it's been endlessly parodied for the military, which of course misses the point Goldsmith made with it. The film was one of seven he scored for director Franklin J Schaffner.

Perhaps their biggest achievement (in every cinematic sense, not just box office) was *Planet Of The Apes* (1968). Science fiction had mostly kept itself to mutant monsters and alien invasions during the 50s. Only occasionally did someone look to craft a social allegory or offer a warning about the future. The 60s were a dry period for science fiction in any form, with only the French seeming to have anything to say with *La Jetée* (1963), *Alphaville* (1965) and *Fahrenheit 451* (1966). Experimental scoring approaches were applied to each from Trevor Duncan, Paul Misraki and Bernard Herrmann respectively. *Planet Of The Apes* also came from a French source (the novel by Pierre Boulle) and gave Goldsmith an opportunity to be more experimental than anyone had yet dared to be. The music is full of harsh and complex rhythms, moans, unique percussion (e.g. kitchen mixing bowls!), blasts of air, echoes and grinding string work. It all supports the backdrop of an arid alien landscape perfectly, bouncing off canyon walls and drifting interminably into an uncertain horizon. For the all-important ape revelation with the cue 'The Hunt,' Goldsmith helped create one of the most visually shocking moments in cinema. Even if the clue was in the title, it is an enormous surprise when a slam zoom across a field of wheat picks out a horseback rider to be a gorilla. The surprise owes much to the build-up of percussion that leads to the bleating of a ram's horn backed by a cuika (an instrument which mimics the "ooh-ooh-ooh" of an ape). One of the most remarkable things about the score is that every effect is achieved acoustically and not electronically. With pop music increasingly dominating the music scene, this was a score to remind the industry it was still possible to be original.

The modernist (atonal yet structured) approach Goldsmith took with *Planet Of The Apes* and later *The Illustrated Man* (1969) also appeared in Leonard Rosenman's *Fantastic Voyage* (1968) and Lalo Schifrin's *THX 1138* (1970). Collectively they showed science fiction to be a genre with intellectual potential. 1968 became the historical marker when it directly influenced the recording industry with Stanley Kubrick's *2001: A Space Odyssey*. A long-lost score by Alex North was resurrected in the 90s by Goldsmith, but the music everyone knows only too well from the film is Richard Strauss' 'Also Sprach Zarathustra.' The piece has become an anthem for countless sporting events, stage shows and comedic spoofs. What happened to North's work is that it was lost to one of the first overt examples of a director falling in love with their temp track (a composite of existing pieces to support a film while being edited). The fact that the classical pieces chosen found enormous favour with the record-buying public would seem to indicate Kubrick made the commercially correct decision. The resultant album successfully crossed both pop and classical charts. It also spawned a sequel album with the awful moniker 'inspired by' that means the music had nothing to do with the film at all.

With similar thinking on *The Graduate* and *Easy Rider*, you can understand why the conventional Golden Age composer had reason to feel somewhat threatened moving into the 70s. The Silver Age meant being free to try new things, but how long would it be before Hollywood won its financially-motivated struggle to turn film music into best-selling chart music?

5. Romance Ain't Dead

The 70s began without any clear sense of identity or belonging. Studio music departments had been dissolved for some time, so composers were roving freelancers. Young new blood was more welcome than ever and existing composers had to hold their ground in the midst of the free-for-all. However, try to find noteworthy soundtracks at the beginning of the decade and you'll see that there had never been a more wretched time for humdrum and miscellany.

There were some standout cult highlights. In 1971, Stanley Kubrick adapted the classics again for *A Clockwork Orange*. The works of Beethoven, Rossini and Elgar on record found nowhere near the level of favour that *2001* had and the film famously died a death of moral outrage. Another expression of social dissatisfaction came in the guise of Jack Carter, Michael Caine's grittiest role in *Get Carter*. The jazzy, harpsichord-laced music from British composer Roy Budd made the vengeful thug seem even tougher. It was a score that found renewed appeal in the late 90s when a series of Budd's work appeared on CD. *Shaft* was another cool cat patrolling the streets that year, backed by a tune that was finger-clicking good. Isaac Hayes won a Best Song Oscar for the single and album that topped US charts.

John Carpenter made his sit-up-and-take-notice debut as director and composer in 1973 with *Dark Star*. His simplistic synthesiser scores would have tremendous impact on a film music scene rapidly falling in love with electronic overlays. The following year David Shire applied the 12-tone method of composition (as mentioned when discussing *The Cobweb*) to the noisy subway heist thriller *The Taking Of Pelham 123*. Then in 1975 came a surreal and kinky reminder that the Musical could still work on the big screen, with the outrageous *Rocky Horror Picture Show*. Visually (and often musically) it followed in the footsteps of the monster flicks of the 50s, but its real legacy was in encouraging audience participation to an unprecedented level. The decade's other *Rocky* came a year later, and introduced beefcake Sylvester Stallone as a boxing champ from the Philadelphia slums. Bill Conti's training montage fanfare is one more instantly recognisable motif to perfectly capture an activity (ring fighting) and an emotion (the loser triumphs). 1976 was also the year of Bernard Herrmann's final score. He'd been one of the composers hit hardest by the move away from earlier musical styles. Sadly he died just as he'd found a comfortable go-between of jazz-fused pop and orchestra for Martin Scorsese's *Taxi Driver*. The tortured saxophone lament which portrays Robert DeNiro's inner pain is a poignant tribute. Not only did he die before hearing his music to film and miss the universal acclaim it received, but if he'd lived on a few years he'd have seen a return of those musical styles and values he deplored the loss of.

Beyond these, there really isn't much more to talk about for the first half of the 70s. Of far more interest was a series of re-recordings that appeared on vinyl as of 1972 under the baton of conductor, producer and film music aficionado Charles Gerhardt. 'The Sea Hawk: The Classic Film Scores Of Erich Wolfgang Korngold' was a phenomenal success, peaking classical charts rapidly. Clearly the record-buying public were keen to hear more than the general wash of pop song collections around at the time. The RCA label followed it with similar collections for Max Steiner, Alfred Newman, Bernard Herrmann, Franz Waxman, Miklós Rózsa, Dimitri Tiomkin, a second Korngold volume and a few celebrity-themed compilations (e.g. Errol Flynn). Other record labels jumped aboard the revival of interest, and film music collectors suddenly found themselves able to actually have a collection! It was a much-needed reminder of the quality output from the Golden Age and most certainly helped the career of one young composer...

The Force Is Strong With This One

Director Steven Spielberg found himself making a temp track for *Sugarland Express* (1974) from two scores by Johnny Williams: *The Reivers* (1969) and *The Cowboys* (1972). They eschewed pop for an orchestra and were in obvious contrast to Williams' more high-profile flirtation with disco and disaster for *The Poseidon Adventure* (1972), *The Towering Inferno* (1974) and *Earthquake* (1974), which used the general style of the day. After their fruitful collaboration on *Sugarland Express,* there was no one better suited to plumb submerged depths of fear for the film which forever changed the way summer movies were conceived. *Jaws* (1975) was more than just the hit of the year. It made so much money that Hollywood was frantic to learn the secret of its success. This was where concept was first considered, and would rapidly lead to the now painfully prevalent concept movie. Its other success the industry sought to replicate was the album and single that proved an orchestral score (and one ostensibly for a horror movie) could scale charts despite strong pop opposition.

Record sales, repeat viewing figures and the Oscar that Williams won all say something about the powerful effect his music had. From the opening point of view shot moving through deep waters, we're made to understand this isn't some holiday diving footage or aquatic documentary. Those low thudding notes leave us in no uncertainty that danger lurks. Britain's Debbie Wiseman told me that "as a film composer you know to avoid that repeated semitone phrase since it is now forever associated with sharks." Several other composers have also remarked that they consciously steer clear of that phrase, which shows how big an impact it has made on the public consciousness.

Two years later, Spielberg introduced Williams to his friend George Lucas, who was working on a science fiction film. Lucas wanted it to have an emotional familiarity since the backdrop of creatures and locales looked so alien. *Star Wars* (1977) is rightly hailed as the Second Coming of film music. Every aspect of the film's release was a genuine phenomenon, coining the word "blockbuster" to describe the unprecedented level of queuing that cinemas experienced for tickets. The two-disc album immediately became the biggest selling non-pop record (at that time), and saw more cover versions and concert performances than anything else in film music history. Fans who complained about the concert suite presentation of the album had to wait until the Special Edition re-release of the film in 1997. Williams has always been perfectly clear about why he re-sequences his albums. "What I usually try to do, which may come from years of making concert programmes, is to make a musical programme based on material I've got from the film that will make the most rewarding listening experience in terms of entr'acte, overture, soft, loud, fast, slow, etc. So there's a gestalt or contour to keep the listener interested."

This level of success and adoration (and another Oscar) doesn't come without good reason. Very simply, the wall-to-wall music is flawless in supporting the on-screen adventure, and in communicating emotions that could easily get lost in the spectacle of visual effects. There is the endlessly copied opening of the enormous Star Destroyer passing overhead. Without Williams' bold march you wouldn't know that the little ship is the good guy. A few minutes later, without the delicate 'Princess Leia Theme' for flute, the scene of her slotting the Death Star plans into R2-D2 could seem like some lady is making toast. Without the adagio (slow) version of the 'Force Theme' as Luke gazes at Tatooine's setting twin suns, he might as well be birdwatching. Without the upbeat, goofy homage to a 1930s Benny Goodman swing band, the Cantina sequence could seem pretty silly with so many papier mâché puppets and rubber masks. The list goes on way beyond this first third of the film of course.

Apart from its jaw-dropping record sales and textbook demonstration of every conceivable way a score can benefit a film, the real success of the music was in convincing studios the late romantic style wasn't completely dead. This was the Golden Age style at its very best, hearkening back to the work of Korngold, Steiner and Rózsa from the 30s and 40s. Romantic is taken as meaning large-scale orchestral music inspired to be written for other than purely musical reasons. It refers to a 19th century of rich harmony, melody and poetry which was exactly what George Lucas wanted so as to be light years away from the disco craze swamping everything else.

There's only ever been one thing wrong with *Star Wars*, and that's the fact it has always completely overshadowed *Close Encounters Of The Third Kind*, which came out the same year. Everyone who's seen it remembers the significance of the spaceship's five-note musical message (which took more than two hundred and fifty attempts to get right for Spielberg). With only a partial reliance on the romantic form, audiences have never embraced it as openly. It may be atonal (not belonging to any key) in places, yet it performs just as important a role in the film as in *Star Wars*. Take away the rushing blasts of noise from the UFO chase around a road bend, and you have an outdoor fireworks display. The film is largely about communication via music, so it would be unthinkable to take away the tuba and synthesiser conversation of the finale from the blinking light show. All in all, there may never have been a more intellectualised consideration of the use of music as an integral part of a film.

Williams' next major project brought science fiction down to Earth with the arrival of the greatest superhero, and the greatest superhero theme. *Superman: The Movie* (1978) features a 'March' of such patriotic pomp it has remained the warm-up of choice for sporting teams the world over. Williams doesn't put a foot wrong in characterising the alien politics of planet Krypton with bells, percussion and synthesiser. Nor the folksy farm life of the Kent family in Smallville, the bustle of city life in Metropolis, the bumbling villainous life of Lex Luthor and Otis, or the love affair with modern gal Lois Lane. Then the composer shot back into space to that faraway galaxy for the sequel adored by all film music fans, *The Empire Strikes Back* (1980). Much speculation surrounds why this should hold more appeal than its bracketing chapters of the trilogy, and even over these other scores mentioned here preceding or following. One answer is that it ends unresolved with several plot threads in peril. Musically that's translated into a much darker overall mood, with the grand 'Imperial March' being at the heart of all that's suddenly discovered to be wrong with the Skywalker family. There are lots of grey areas in the score, such as the brass rumble putting a question mark over the head of bounty hunter Boba Fett, the insinuation by strings of pure evil in the swamp cave when Luke confronts his fears, and the consistently subtle tricks (such as noticeable rare absences of music) creating an air of something amiss at turncoat Lando Calrissian's Cloud City. It's tempting to ignore *Return Of The Jedi*, which followed 3 years later, since it devolved into a regurgitation of material (some literally reused from *Star Wars*) for a display of Muppets and teddy bears. Luke's emotional arc story should have remained at the forefront of things, but does at least get a satisfying pay-off scored with the first use of chorus in the trilogy, giving the final lightsabre duel a quasi-religious feel. Musically and visually it's an anticlimax to what was built up, but this space opera does make for nearly 6 hours of the very best of Williams' career.

Look At The Size Of These Things

In several circles of fandom, a line of dialogue from *Star Wars* has been cheerily adapted to sum-up the composer's influence as the 70s became the 80s: "Do not underestimate the power of John Williams." Incredibly, having mentioned all these enormously popular successes so far, there are still two more. More incredible is that in between he still had time to knock off accompaniment to Alfred Hitchcock's final movie *Family Plot* (1976), and a march for *Midway* (1976) that often finds itself in concert repertoires. *Jaws 2* (1978) expanded all the terror of the original, while *The Fury* (1978) had an over-the-top psychological waltz. He was the first to suggest *Dracula* (1979) was a misunderstood romantic, and then gave Spielberg a comedic spark for *1941* (1979), Spielberg's only real misfire. It is to Spielberg we turn again for the last two blockbusters that round out Williams' decade-long reign.

If *Superman* is the ultimate superhero theme, then *Raiders Of The Lost Ark* (1981) is the ultimate adventurer theme. Indiana Jones instantly became a box-office smash and another best-selling album. Throughout the film, there are examples of music working exactly the way it should. Pizzicato (plucked) strings give you the creeps as hundreds of tarantulas drop onto the archaeologist's shoulders. The orchestra Mickey-Mouses his mad dash from the temple when everything starts falling apart, culminating in brass intonements of doom as a giant rock chases him before everything comes to a deafening crash of silence. The crowd-pleasing fanfare serves as a musical punchline to reinforce a joke about him being scared of a snake after everything that's just happened. Again, this is only a demonstration covering the early part of the film. Later comes the awe-filled Ark theme, a love theme for Marion, and one of cinema's best action cues for one of cinema's best action scenes as Jones single-handedly takes out a truck convoy of Nazi troops. There's no dialogue for almost 10 minutes, making it a gift for the composer to act as narrator, telling us where everyone is at any given moment, and reassuring us that the hero will come through in the end. A pair of sequels followed; *Indiana Jones And The Temple Of Doom* (1984) and *Indiana Jones And The Last Crusade* (1989), but by a shift in tone neither fully recaptured the exuberance of the original.

The final 80s treasure (and Oscar) with Spielberg was *ET: The Extra-Terrestrial* (1982). It was another massive album seller, again conforming to Williams' preference for concert arrangements of the principal themes (one of which was a singles chart success too). Like each of these blockbusters highlighted, it was reissued on an expanded CD. More than any of the others it splits fan opinion as to whether suites or chronological order best suit his albums. Sentimentality is *ET*'s general mood, playing on the heartstrings of every child who had an imaginary friend, alien or otherwise. Once familiar with the film, anyone following the music can't help but be drawn toward the astounding 15-minute bike chase finale, which brims over with up-tempo cheer. *ET* by no means brought any kind of an end to this period of grandeur, but none of what followed in the 80s ever attained the same heights of popularity. While some would prove downright forgettable, at least there was *The River* (1984), *SpaceCamp* (1986), *The Witches Of Eastwick* (1987), *Empire Of The Sun* (1987), *The Accidental Tourist* (1988), *Born On The Fourth Of July* (1989) and *Always* (1989). Shifting records off shelves, encouraging repeat cinema viewings and persuading the romantic idiom back into film music make Williams a principal architect in this period of big-screen history.

It took a decade from *2001: A Space Odyssey* to *Star Wars* for the industry to trust science fiction as a genre of legitimate financial worth. As always when Hollywood latched upon something, it was then rapidly done to excess. TV rushed out several projects, of which the most successful pair featured strong orchestral backing from Stu Philips. In 1979, both *Buck Rogers In The 25th Century* and *Battlestar Galactica* found themselves being touched up for theatrical release in the UK. John Barry aided Disney's bid for sci-fi glory with *The Black Hole* (1979), and Elmer Bernstein experimented seriously for *Saturn 3* (1980), in animated fashion for *Heavy Metal* (1981), then with tongue firmly in cheek for the hijinks of *Spacehunter: Adventures In The Forbidden Zone* (1983). Other big names asked to work symphonic magic into semi-serious sci-fi included: Miklós Rózsa for HG Wells' romance in 70s San Francisco in *Time After Time* (1979), Laurence Rosenthal for a late bid in the disaster genre with *Meteor* (1979), Ennio Morricone inexplicably replicated director John Carpenter's style for shock masterpiece *The Thing* (1982), and Henry Mancini did his best to rescue the limp hybrid of space vampires in *Lifeforce* (1985).

Star Wars-inspired orchestral backing was used in most genres at the start of the 80s. Science fiction was the main genre to explore the burgeoning muscial capabilities of electronics. Rock and New Age transmitted itself into space courtesy of Queen for the camp glitz of *Flash Gordon* (1980). John Carpenter gave us a hard-as-nails anthem for Snake Plissken in *Escape From New York* (1981). Also Vangelis suggested tranquil in ignorance for the bleak future of *Blade Runner* (1982), and Wendy Carlos eased us into the digital realm with *Tron* (1982). Brad Fiedel thumped metallic footfalls beneath Arnold Schwarzenegger's breakthrough as *The Termin*ator (1984), and Toto (and Brian Eno) made thoughts and emotions as openly apparent as the vast deserts of *Dune* (1984). Maurice Jarre showed he was one of the main synthesiser composers of the time for *Enemy Mine* (1985), and Harold Faltermeyer put a beat into step aerobics with 'Captain Freedom's Workout' when Schwarzenegger switched into good guy mode as *The Running Man* (1987). There's a bigger list, but these are enough to illustrate just how arbitrary the studios were with their choice of composer and musical style despite Williams' trend-setting.

There Is Another

Like Williams, Jerry Goldsmith was enormously prolific during the 70s into the 80s. He applied impressionistic techniques to the scores for *Logan's Run* (1976), *Damnation Alley* (1977) and *Capricorn One* (1978), which is to say their music did not belong to any one character or emotional story arc, but instead followed the drama itself. 1979 was the year of his main contribution to the science fiction genre though. First came Ridley Scott's *Alien*, for which every conceivable aspect of production lived up to the title. From the nightmarish organic look of the aliens and their environment designed by Swiss artist HR Giger to the heavily industrialised vision of future habitat, it was a spectacle as original on the eye as *Star Wars*. On top of that sits possibly the coldest of scores ever written for a film. As a stand-alone album, it is background music for a haunted house. It breathes and it sighs (an echoing four-note phrase for woodwinds pinched for countless subsequent scores), then screams and beats the walls with innovative percussion effects (e.g. log drums). Not only did it set a template for the three movies that followed, but also for endless rip-offs and pastiches. Even more popular from the same year is what many consider to be Goldsmith's finest work: *Star Trek: The Motion Picture*. The Star Trek franchise had been mothballed a decade earlier, but new possibilities in special effects were too promising for Paramount to ignore.

Anyone who thought the elaborate visuals overstayed their welcome nicknamed it "The Slow Motion Picture." Paradoxically, the two key sequences this complaint is attributed to are also the musical highlights. Number one occurs as Admiral Kirk is ferried to the newly refitted Enterprise. It's most certainly a case of showing off the special effects, but the 6 minutes are made into a majestic ballet of movement by Goldsmith's glorious music. It builds to a huge crescendo to illustrate Kirk's pride when he sees the ship head on, and leaves us in no uncertainty that he needs to get out more. The second sequence is the far longer one when they enter the V'ger cloud. Here the composer almost seems to adapt Herrmann's emotional vortex from *Vertigo* with an unresolving cyclic motif perfectly capturing the open-mouthed crew. Lots of creative effects are dropped on top of this sense of awe. Of particular importance is the Blaster Beam, a seventeen-foot metal bar strung with bridge cables and spanked, which is the cloud's unique leitmotivic device. There's only the vaguest of references to the original 60s TV series theme by Alexander Courage, who assisted orchestrating the score. (See Chapter 7 for an explanation of technical phrases.) Goldsmith's own theme has gone on to be adapted for the *Star Trek: The Next Generation* TV series theme, then reused in *Star Trek V: The Final Frontier* (1989), *Star Trek: First Contact* (1996) and *Star Trek: Insurrection* (1998). Proving just how respected this was, he also composed the main title theme for TV's *Star Trek: Voyager*. In total, it's a body of work that makes him more prominent in the genre than any other composer.

Goldsmith was also at the forefront of sci-fi genre crossovers. He scored rugged menace for the *High Noon*-in-space, *Outland* (1981). He made his own bid for superhero success with a soaring fanfare for *Supergirl* (1984). There was an experiment in electronics for the killer robots of *Runaway* (1984). He captured the daydreaming of every schoolboy for *Explorers* (1985), and kinetic comedy for the biology lesson of *Innerspace* (1987). These last two were for director Joe Dante, with whom Goldsmith has had another long-standing working relationship. It began in 1983 with the anthology of stories for *Twilight Zone: The Movie*, to which Dante contributed a segment. As a genre crossover, it fully utilised Goldsmith's versatility as the composer who also led the field in the world of horror. Dante immediately secured him for his breakthrough movie *Gremlins* (1984). It blurred the lines between film categories - part chiller, part comedy, but mostly cute.

What had really changed the horror genre permanently (winning Goldsmith his only Oscar to date) was *The Omen* (1976). Instead of glossing over or cutting away from gruesome deaths the film was graphically direct, raising censorship issues lasting to present day. Musically it was a watershed in stylistic association. The choral black mass ('Ave Satani') has become a template for anyone looking to depict demonic activity. It's often been mistaken for Carl Orff's 'Carmina Burana,' yet here in its original setting the effect is genuinely unnerving. Goldsmith adapted and occasionally bettered the material in the two sequels *Damien: Omen II* (1978) and *The Final Conflict* (1981). More than any other composer, he seems comfortable to stick around as studios try re-bottling box-office lightning. Finishing the *Omen* series he moved straight on to *Poltergeist* (1982), which is another of his most respected works. It's a score of frightening contradictions. A fragile beauty pervades the lullaby for Carol Anne, the little girl kidnapped by ghosts, and it speaks to the tragedy tearing apart a suburbanite family. Then there are shocking bursts of dissonance and harsh textural elements for the supernatural pyrotechnics, such as whenever the clown toy appears. The dismal *Poltergeist II: The Other Side* (1986) followed. Rounding out his work in the 80s house of horror was the inevitable *Psycho II* (1983) for which he wisely avoided any possible comparison with Herrmann's seminal score.

Outside of the two principal fantasy genres, Goldsmith excelled in everything else just as memorably. *Chinatown* (1974) remains his personal favourite, perhaps as a mark of proud accomplishment having been written in a ridiculously short 10 days. The romantic trumpet solos defined film noir better than anything in the genre's 50s heyday, and is a subject of study in many film music classes. *The Wind And The Lion* (1975) is the best example of the composer's trademark brand of powerhouse action writing, here lent Arabic rhythmic structure. The cue 'Raisuli Attacks' is one of the most ferocious pieces of music ever written for film, and makes the sequence of a horseback sword duel thunderously exhilarating. To these can be added: saucy humour for *The First Great Train Robbery* (1979), fluttering brass stings for another late disaster entry with *The Swarm* (1978), Wagnerian high adventure for the Indiana Jones wannabe *King Solomon's Mines* (1985), and a sign that there might be a sense of humour at work with numerous self-parodies for Joe Dante's *The 'burbs* (1989).

Throughout the 80s, audiences were hammered over the head with attempts to create superstar personas, and no one helped Sylvester Stallone achieve that more than Goldsmith with his scores for the testosterone-dripping *Rambo* trilogy. The music goes from plaintive melancholy (with outbursts of muscular brass) in *First Blood* (1982), to grizzled patriotism in *Rambo: First Blood Part II* (1985), to all-out orchestral war in tutti (all playing simultaneously) fashion for *Rambo III* (1988). Never let it be said Hollywood won't squeeze something for all it's worth.

He Was But A Learner

Producer/director Roger Corman diverted James Horner from aspiring toward a concert hall career, and dropped *Battle Beyond The Stars* (1980) in his lap. Clearly designed to cash in on *Star Wars*, and also clearly temp tracked with music from Goldsmith's *Star Trek*, it was nonetheless a massive feather in Horner's cap. To prove it, director Nicholas Meyer ignored the borrowings and signed him up to do better on *Star Trek II: The Wrath Of Khan* (1982). Full of nautical allusions to creator Gene Roddenberry's vision of Horatio Hornblower in space, this is robust music of epic proportions. The antithesis of his own beautiful new Enterprise theme is the chaotic motif for Khan's wrath, a whiplashing series of cracks and brass wails. There's subtle underscore for the death of Spock, eerie percussive and electronic effect for 'Khan's Pets,' and non-stop high-spirited invention for the taut strategic game of hide and seek at the 'Battle In The Mutara Nebula.' Leonard Nimoy retained Horner for his directorial debut on the next instalment in the series, *Star Trek III: The Search For Spock* (1984), which toned the action right down in favour of a character study on ageing and pseudo-spiritualism.

Elsewhere in the genre Horner proved equally capable. *Krull* (1983) didn't know whether it was science fiction, Tolkien fantasy or swashbuckler. Assuming it wanted to be all of the above, the score masterfully wove each appropriate style together. With tips of the hat to the classics of Holst and Prokofiev, it's an early example of how Horner happily deconstructs existing works for the construction of his own. Talking of which, Horner often reuses themes from his *Brainstorm* score of the same year. *Cocoon* (1985) didn't actually require any fantastical elements, but he did get to indulge in a passion for big band writing (also in the 1988 sequel, *Cocoon: The Return*). More than his other work in the genre, *Aliens* (1986) became the one to set trends. Despite shades of Khachaturian and Goldsmith, Horner's brand of militaria has often appeared in films depicting US Marines in gung-ho mode. The cue 'Resolution' was used in dozens of movie trailers, as well as inexplicably reappearing for the finale of *Die Hard* two years later.

In the horror realm he suggested a native history to the lycanthropic tale of *Wolfen* (1981), made the sheer daftness of Michael Caine's dismemberment vaguely believable for *The Hand* (1981), and brought heartfelt magic to the dark fantasy ride of *Something Wicked This Way Comes* (1983). He kept things nice and funky for Eddie Murphy in *48 Hrs.* (1982), and electronically mimicked Schwarzenegger's thudding footfalls in *Commando* (1985) and *Red Heat* (1988). He ignored the anachronism of synthesisers underlining Christian Slater's 14th-Century loss of virginity in *The Name Of The Rose* (1986), and scored the ultimate tearjerker motif for Hollywood's infatuation with the line "I love you Dad" in *Field Of Dreams* (1989). He also patriotically paved the way for every black male actor subsequently accepted in the 90s by Hollywood in the late racial apology movie *Glory* (1989).

Keeping the kids happy on Saturday mornings, Horner was instrumental in one of the first non-Disney animated ventures with *An American Tail* (1986), especially with the highly popular song 'Somewhere Out There.' *Willow* (1988) wasn't the start of his relationship with director Ron Howard (*Cocoon* was), but the opulent wall-to-wall swashbuckle he provided ensured he'd be the composer Howard would return to more than any other. Subsequently they've collaborated on *Apollo 13* (1995), *Ransom* (1996) and *How The Grinch Stole Christmas* (2000). His last children's film in the 80s would provide grist to the mill of all naysayers who disagree with his technique of reusing material. *Honey, I Shrunk The Kids* (1989) landed Disney with a lawsuit claiming one of Horner's main themes bore uncanny resemblance to a tune by Raymond Scott (the great Warner Brothers cartoon maestro).

A Million Voices Cried Out In Terror

Most composers agree that all music is deconstruction anyway, and by turning now to the boom of the horror genre from the 70s into the 80s, that should be very apparent. We've touched on the A-list scores from the triumvirate of Williams, Goldsmith and Horner. Little of their work stemmed from Hollywood's exploitative agenda however. *The Omen* was cited as the first mainstream showcase of gore, but the underground circuit naturally beat it. For instance, George A Romero's original *Night Of The Living Dead* was 1968. The gruesome zombie film appeared from nowhere during a period that was mostly concerned with commercial efforts and teen fodder. Hollywood soon sank its teeth into horror movies for all their exploitative worth, but nowhere near as deeply as independent studios. Early milestones include director Wes Craven's debut *Last House On The Left* (1972), faith-testing shocker *The Exorcist* (1973) which famously used Mike Oldfield's 'Tubular Bells,' and *The Texas Chainsaw Massacre* (1974) with teeth-grating electronic sound design.

Horror movies require musical sleight of hand more than any other. For these 2 decades, electronic howls, squeals, icicle drips and screams did the job because keyboards and anything electronically off the wall were in. In Italy, director Dario Argento worked with rock band Goblin for a screaming soundtrack to *Deep Red* aka *Profondo Rosso* (1975) and *Suspiria* (1976). The mainstream proliferation of sequencers and synths came with John Carpenter's runaway success on *Halloween* (1978). The score came fast and cheap, because he was the composer too. His extremely simple main theme (based on a bongo warm-up exercise) has been one of the most imitated phrases of all time. For an early example, seek out Fred Myrow's music for *Phantasm* from the following year.

There were many keyboard contributions to controversial projects of the day: *Dawn Of The Dead* (Goblin again), *I Spit On Your Grave, The Hills Have Eyes* (all 1978) and *The Driller Killer* (1979). An occasional orchestral effort found its way into the genre such as Elmer Bernstein's tongue-in-cheek work on *An American Werewolf In London* (1981). The 80s otherwise happily circumnavigated higher budgets with young, keen and inexpensive composers looking for a break. Director Sam Raimi gave one to aspiring musician Joseph LoDuca on *The Evil Dead* (1983). The atmospheres created on and off screen between them have kept them working together ever since in film (sequels *Evil Dead 2* (1987) and *Army Of Darkness* (1993)) and TV (*Hercules, Xena* and *American Gothic*). Dario Argento kept the cult circuit undead by letting British composer Simon Boswell contribute cues to *Demons* (1985) and *Demons 2* (1987) before tackling the whole of *Deliria* (1987). Guitarist Richard Band made his presence felt in cult horror with *The House On Sorority Row* (1983) and *Re-Animator* (1985) where he laced a beat into Herrmann's *Psycho* title music to allow the film's excesses to be perceived as black comedy.

The 80s were a breeding ground for horror franchises, which in musical terms almost never meant development of thematic material. *Chainsaw Massacre* was the first splatter movie to spawn a sequel for its dubiously iconic villain. Then *Halloween* kept Michael Myers alive indefinitely via Carpenter. Harry Manfredini had the task of resurrecting Jason Vorhees in seven of the eight *Friday The 13th* movies begun in 1980. There was no such consistency for Freddy Krueger however, who after being introduced via Charles Bernstein's tinkling lullaby in *A Nightmare On Elm Street* (1984), would be passed between Christopher Young, Angelo Badalamenti, Craig Safan, Jay Ferguson, Brian May and J Peter Robinson. Young redeemed himself for *Freddy's Dead* however with the two 80s Pinhead movies *Hellraiser* (1987) and *Hellbound: Hellraiser II* (1988). Both are full of gothic romanticism, but the second breaks all manner of ground with snarling energy and an orchestra bleating out G-O-D in Morse Code!

One of the biggest success stories was Stephen King, from whom Hollywood couldn't obtain book rights fast enough after Brian De Palma's adaptation of *Carrie* (1976). It was a box-office smash thanks to that most famous of double-whammy endings, and the crafty misdirection of Italian composer Pino Donaggio's delicate flute theme ripped apart by brass and bells for the surprise. Then came Kubrick to once again shake things up with an amalgam of musical sources for the slow-burning fuse of Jack Nicholson's performance in *The Shining* (1980). The anthology collection *Creepshow* (1982) allowed John Harrison to play horror for laughs, while Charles Bernstein accentuated every snarl and howl of bad dog *Cujo* (1983). David Cronenberg had to work without his regular collaborator Howard Shore for studio reasons on *The Dead Zone* (1983), but in doing so launched the career of Michael Kamen with his sorrowful music for haunted psychic Johnny. John Carpenter used keyboards and guitar to keep killer car *Christine* (1983) alive, and Jonathan Elias used a children's choir to keep the spirit of the fields dead in *Children Of The Corn* (1984). The decade went on with lots more electronic terror for *Firestarter* (1984) by Tangerine Dream, *Cat's Eye* (1985) by Alan Silvestri, *Silver Bullet* (1985) by Jay Chattaway, and the one and only time King would try his hand at directing with *Maximum Overdrive* (1986) by AC/DC.

We're Caught In A Tractor Beam

In 1977, Paramount Pictures kept cash registers ringing by capitalising on the disco craze with *Saturday Night Fever*. They had entrusted a music industry executive (Robert Stigwood) to produce the film on the assumption that he would know how to tap into contemporary culture. It was the biggest-selling album of all time with 25 million sales internationally. It was mass-marketed and made the Bee Gees an even bigger phenomenon than they already were. It also catapulted John Travolta into stardom. When it was seen that a star could draw the public into cinemas and record stores for disco, they tried it again with 50s rock in *Grease* (1978), and then Country in *Urban Cowboy* (1980).

If the Musical could be popular once more on the big screen, then it was possible on the smaller screen too. The answer was the MTV channel launched in the summer of 1981. It was an immediate melting pot for artistic creativity. Firstly for music, but also in the areas of directing and editing technique on the video format. Movie studios therefore sought to take something back, and began to poach video and commercials directors.

After the success of disco, studios turned to dance in 1980 where the do-it-for-fun *The Blues Brothers* contrasted with the do-it-for-art *Fame* (which spawned a TV show from 1982 to 1987). Commercials director Adrian Lyne then raised the bar with *Flashdance* (1983). Everyone agreed it was one long rock video, and featured one of the first credits for a music supervisor, who oversaw Giorgio Moroder's score and songs. Dance stayed in everyone's mind with Kevin Bacon's turn the same year in *Footloose*, and a few years later with the sleeper hit *Dirty Dancing* (1987). Their albums were massive chart hits, and initiated a public taste for song compilations that has lasted far longer than the songs' period of popularity in the late 60s. One major factor influencing record buying and marketing trends was the emergence of compact disc technology. The first player debuted in 1980, and then the Philips and Sony Corporations began to make them commercially available in 1985. Vinyl successes on the cusp of the CD market and born out of the MTV era were generally sold on the basis of one or two songs going to Number 1 in the charts. For the years in question, these successes were: *The Big Chill* (1983) with

Marvin Gaye's 'I Heard It Through The Grapevine,' *Ghostbusters* (1984) with Ray Parker Jr.'s title song, *Against All Odds* (1984) with Phil Collins' 'Take A Look At Me Now,' *The Woman In Red* (1984) with Stevie Wonder's 'I Just Called To Say I Love You,' *Purple Rain* (1984) with Prince's Oscar-winning title song, and *White Nights* (1985) with Lionel Richie's 'Say You, Say Me.'

The studios were determined to mine the disposable income of teenagers. As an alternative to creating movie icons, they poached pop superstars like Prince, who was followed into the cinema by Madonna with *Desperately Seeking Susan*. Teen flicks were never more popular than when conceptualised and marketed by someone who could tap into pop culture with ease. Foremost among those making the attempt was writer/producer/director John Hughes. His films of the mid-80s are a perfect snapshot of fashion, language and musical tastes. Titles were inspired by songs and vice versa. Their compilation song albums completely ignored scores by Ira Newborn. This was exactly what the industry had been moving towards, hence the sizeable box office of *Sixteen Candles* in 1984, *The Breakfast Club* and *Weird Science* (which gave Danny Elfman's band Oingo Boingo their only Number 1 hit) in 1985, and *Ferris Bueller's Day Off* and *Pretty In Pink* (both 1986).

The multitask role of Hughes across this series of films illustrates the shift in power behind the scenes that came out of the disco movie producer's success. Studios were looking for blockbusters, not artistic visions. So stand up Steven Spielberg for showing the way with the start of a secondary producer role that put his name before a director's in a film title. 1985 was the key year when 'Steven Spielberg Presents' *Back To The Future*, *The Goonies* and *Young Sherlock Holmes*. Part of that role was to ensure subsidiary income in soundtrack sales, and so the scores by Alan Silvestri, Dave Grusin and Bruce Broughton respectively took a back seat to songs from Huey Lewis And The News and Cindy Lauper for the first two, but no soundtrack at all for the third.

As corporations began buying each other out (e.g. Sony bought Columbia), the shift from director to producer on designer blockbuster movies soon became apparent. Wearing similar (but only slightly smaller) shoes was Joel Silver, who since the mid-80s has been responsible for two *Predator*s, three *Die Hard*s, four *Lethal Weapon*s, *Commando* (1985), *Road House* (1989), *Demolition Man* (1993) and *The Matrix* (1999). The other pair of names to facilitate the elevation of the producer, the development of the concept movie and help generate the Planet Hollywood-styled star icon was Jerry Bruckheimer and Don Simpson.

They gave us *Flashdance* and *Beverly Hills Cop*, then stuck a pair of cool shades on Tom Cruise for the whole of *Top Gun* in 1986 (Best Song Oscar for Georgio Moroder's 'Take My Breath Away') and later for *Days Of Thunder* (1990). Bruckheimer went on to produce a series of movies that all feature scores stemming from the direction electronic music was taking in the 80s (*Bad Boys* (1995), *The Rock* (1996), *Con Air* (1997), *Armageddon* (1998), *Enemy Of The State* (1998) and *Gone In Sixty Seconds* (2000)). Outside the horror genre, there was the occasional successful use of synthesisers and sequencers in unexpected places: Vangelis' Oscar-winning *Chariots Of Fire* (1981), Japanese composer Ryuichi Sakamoto's melodic *Merry Christmas, Mr Lawrence* (1983), and Maurice Jarre's most popular work away from an orchestra for *Witness* (1985). One of the flash-in-the-pan names of the time was Harold Faltermeyer with *Beverly Hills Cop* (1984, and *II* in 1987), *Fletch* (1985, and *Fletch Lives* in 1989), *Top Gun* (1986), *The Running Man* (1987) and *Tango And Cash* (1989). There was also the German collective Tangerine Dream applying their distinctive brand of ambient electronics to *Risky Business* and *The Keep* in 1983, *Firestarter* (1984), *Fright Night* (1985), the American version of *Legend* in 1985 (it featured a lush Jerry Goldsmith score everywhere else) and *Near Dark* (1987).

Right at the end of the decade came *Black Rain* (1989), the score to have more impact on the increasing number of high concept action movies in the 90s than is generally recognised. "It was pretty out there for its time," admits German composer Hans Zimmer. "But it really shaped the action genre from there on. It suddenly became the temp score for everybody else's action movies. That became really tough on me because the next time I was given an action movie I literally had to try to reinvent the language. Everybody had been following it, so what was new then suddenly became a cliché." The blend of orchestral and made-to-order synthesiser performances works at a very surface level in the film, and has become one of few ways a film composer can hope to be heard in a modern sound mix. This was the beginning of the Media Ventures action style, who are discussed in the next chapter.

Zimmer had lobbied hard for the chance to work with Ridley Scott, and the hard-hitting fusion sound that resulted impressed Scott enough for them to form the most recurring musical relationship in the director's career. Subsequently they collaborated on *Thelma And Louise* (1991), *Gladiator* (2000) and *Hannibal* (2001).

Their Energy Surrounds Us And Binds Us

Long-lasting director/composer relationships are quite simply one of the last places for artistic expression and development. With the takeover of a producer's role, it requires a director's friendship with a composer to ensure musical concepts end up on the screen as originally envisioned. So it is well worth noting the significant friendships forged in the 80s.

David Cronenberg's films are wholly self-contained; yet seem to belong together in a very private universe. Keeping them stylistically individual yet intellectually unified is the director's musical other half, Howard Shore. "When we started, we didn't have a lot of preconceptions," Shore explains. "He was the first director I had worked with, and I was the first composer he had worked with. David doesn't try to steer you or corrupt you in any way. He just wants you to be able to write to the max. That's how we've always worked. It's actually a rare kind of situation to be in. His stuff has always been my most forward thinking." Their projects have been some of the most controversial and stimulating cinematic experiences of the last 20 years, beginning with *The Brood* (1980). Shore worked with a dozen strings to invoke uncertainty and unease for a tale of homicidal mutant babies. Mutants then populated *Scanners* (1981), this time dabbling in pre-synthesiser electronics. Two years on, the composer was ready to go wild with electronic experimentation, distorting voices and building unique effects for *Videodrome*, a strange reaction to the new MTV generation. Their biggest commercial success together was a remake of *The Fly* (1986) starring Jeff Goldblum. Grand operatic tragedy musically surrounds the doomed scientist's disintegration. Along with *Dead Ringers'* poignant expression of suicidal depression in 1988, these two films are the most melodic their music's ever been.

Michael Nyman is often credited with being the first composer to apply minimalism to mainstream film scoring. This is a technique largely concerned with repetition, whereby the speed of cycling material shifts, while the pitch generally doesn't. Whereas Philip Glass seemed to be merely writing his concert works for others to film around (as with the hypnotic *Koyaanisqatsi* in 1983), minimalism's greatest prominence, and Nyman's rising star was in the films of fellow Brit Peter Greenaway. *The Draughtsman's Contract* (1982) featured a dry, clinical portrait of characters lost in portrait painting. Exacting approaches were also applied to both *A Zed And Two Noughts* (1985) and *The Belly Of An Architect* (1987), before a surprise mutual appreciation of Mozart offered something gracefully different for *Drowning By Numbers* (1988) *The Cook, The Thief, His Wife And Her Lover* (1989) both visually and musically split audiences between absolute love or hate of its sensory assault.

Also from the UK came Kenneth Branagh and Patrick Doyle with *Henry V* (1989). This brave debut offered itself up for comparison with that of Sirs Laurence Olivier and William Walton, and came away with a dignified amount of respect. For Scottish composer Doyle, it was a cine-matic baptism of fire with the large-scale symphonic score. "It's a very relaxed relationship," he maintains. "Generally speaking, once he's talked about what he's after in terms of style, we're set. Ken likes a tune and that's really the barometer for the rest of a film for him. He's happy for the rest to develop once we've set a main core. There's been a strong shorthand from the word go. We've got on very well as personalities go. The main priority is having fun. Otherwise what's the point?" Their fun continued by breaking into Hollywood and plunging the depths of Film Noir for *Dead Again* (1991), then getting a tan on the set of *Much Ado About Nothing* (1993) with Doyle's hearty on-screen singing building the cast up for a joyous choral finale.

The most singular pairing to have come from France in the last 30 years is director Luc Besson and composer Eric Serra. *The Last Battle* (1983) was their first big-screen effort, and bore all the hallmarks of working together on student films, with saxophone and synth rock back-ing a samurai warrior cleaning up after a nuclear apocalypse. Then came the home turf hit of *Subway* (1985), launching the career of Christopher Lambert as an eccentric hero hiding from a criminal underworld in the Paris Metro. Serra's upbeat pop score tapped directly into the contempo-rary youth sensibility rebelling against Hollywood conformity. A gentle change of pace for *The Big Blue* (1988) was exactly what the director wanted for his very personal deep-sea diving story, but on this one Holly-wood got its way by replacing Serra's subterranean samples with a more traditional score by Bill Conti for the US market.

Making bigger cross-cultural waves was the mainstream debut of con-troversial Dutch director Paul Verhoeven. Like anyone else breathing, he'd been enormously impressed with the score for *Conan The Barbarian* (1982), with its pagan operatic extremes and memorable melodies. Com-poser Basil Poledouris was born in America of Greek descent, and that West European sensibility shines through many rhythmic licks in his work as well as a bottomless supply of beautiful romantic material (e.g. the tenderness expressed in *The Blue Lagoon* from 1980). Verhoeven wanted all senses of romance to accompany his decadent mediaeval wallow in rape and rabies with *Flesh And Blood* (1985). He got that and more, and the friendship took them on to the big-budget hit *Robocop* (1987), where the industrialised tone of the music suits the cold characters and colder sardonic wit of the plot perfectly. Later they reunited for wry military exercises and satire in *Starship Troopers* (1997).

Of all modern directors, David Lynch is respected as the most aurally attuned. He not only acts as sound designer and mixer, but frequently contributes to the score as well. "What makes it different with David is that he loves music so much," claims composer Angelo Badalamenti. "He finds that the pace and mood of it sometimes dictate the pace of the scene he's going to shoot. I write a lot of music before he even shoots. This is very interesting because in film 99% of the time a composer is brought in at the last moment once there's a director's cut. That gives enough to start composing themes, and before you know it there's a locked picture. Then the composer marries things together. Part of David's genius is that he sees through music. Which is kind of cool, and you can't say that about many people." Their memorable first collaboration was for *Blue Velvet* (1986). It integrated the 50s title song into the fabric of the narrative, demonstrating Lynch's personalised technique of using music as an emotional narrator to tie scenes and character relationships together. Their own song 'Mysteries Of Love' features three times in different forms highlighting the maturation of Kyle Maclachlan's boy-to-man journey. Both 'In Dreams' by Roy Orbison and 'Love Letters' by Victor Young (yes, the Young from Chapter 2) and performed by Kitty Lester take on nightmarish significance when applied to Dennis Hopper's role. Tying the director's 50s sensibilities together is Badalamenti's symphonic score, which began their almost telepathically intuitive working method with one another. The *Twin Peaks* TV Series, super sexy/violent *Wild At Heart* (1990) and unapologetically surreal *Twin Peaks: Fire Walk With Me* (1992) all followed, crowning them as a rare cinematic musical force for cinema of the 90s.

Director Tim Burton and composer Danny Elfman have enjoyed a rich working relationship since the mid-80s. *Pee Wee's Big Adventure* (1985) was a dizzying splash of colour and style with a musical accompaniment that's part Georges Delerue, part Nino Rota, part Bernard Herrmann, but as we would soon discover, all Elfman. "I used to see him in clubs when I wasn't even in the film industry," remembers the director. "They (Elfman's band Oingo Boingo) were very theatrical and fun, and they had a subtext under them being sort of narrative. Not like film music exactly, but there was something in them that seemed very filmic. So when I had the opportunity to make a movie there was no question that it would be great to ask him. He'd been successful in a band, but when we went to the film we were both starting out at the same time. It felt very contemporary to have somebody who was like me in the sense that we knew what we were doing but we didn't know what we were doing. It was new and we were stupid and arrogant to think that we could do it. It was funny to see him in clubs and then dealing with a big orchestra for the first time." *Pee Wee's Big Adventure*'s influence on comedy scoring was instantaneous, and is still felt today. Reinventing themselves completely they returned with the supernaturally screwball *Beetlejuice* (1988), where Elfman mixed Harry Belafonte into his offbeat take on the afterlife. Then everything changed with *Batman* (1989).

The marketing machine set in motion for the Caped Crusader's adventure was at an unprecedented level. It included Warner Brothers securing Prince, one of Warner Music's biggest-selling artists, to write several songs. His album was labelled 'Original Soundtrack'; it preceded the release of the film, and sent one of many songs not actually in the movie ('Batdance') to Number 1. Film studio/record label handshakes inspired by the success of this have led to the current state of affairs, where the word soundtrack means any of a number of things to the public. What hasn't helped is the scenario Elfman faced, whereby his score album was suppressed until a month after the film opened so as not to interfere with Prince's sales. He faced it again the following year on *Dick Tracy*, and has done several times since, as have all too many of his fellow composers. The great shame of this is that his gothic masterpiece sold in undeservedly small numbers and was passed over for Oscar consideration.

Burton and Elfman learned their lesson in corporate commercialism, and played a hand outside of the industry game with their next project. It is with *Edward Scissorhands* (1990) that we now turn to the 90s…

6. Millennium Falcons

...where attention spans are assumed to be so fleeting that trends last mere months. *Edward Scissorhands* is about as personal as any director has allowed themselves to get, being the tale of a misunderstood artist who fears destroying what he touches. Elfman's response has sent influential ripples through the music industry ever since. Its use of wordless chorus seems to have charmed the pants off anyone making a fairy tale on the big screen or small, anything suggesting purity of love, and numerous commercials ranging from cars to cosmetics. It has subsequently become a staple of his own work too. The immediate follow-up with Burton was an attempt to beat Hollywood at its own game with *Batman Returns* (1992). Not only did they avoid demands for marketable pop tunes (Elfman co-wrote one song with Siouxsie And The Banshees), but in both tone and music they ignored the youth market completely. Later they broke genre barriers with the stop-motion animated Musical *The Nightmare Before Christmas* (1993), to which the composer's songwriting skills were of the most important type of narrative function. The kooky style of the songs and score have featured in many trailers and children's films since. 50s-styled sci-fi heyday hokum followed with *Mars Attacks!* (1996), and then 50s-styled Hammer horror hokum with *Sleepy Hollow* (1999).

Only one break occurred in Burton's relationship with Elfman, and that was for *Ed Wood* (1994). For this, the 50s-based B-movie hokum was passed to composer Howard Shore. Bongos, theremin and a touching extract of 'Swan Lake' remind us of Bela Lugosi's era of stardom, when his 1931 *Dracula* was a little early for a score of its own. Shore kept up just as diverse a track record as Burton and Elfman in the 90s by his ongoing partnership with David Cronenberg. Their *Naked Lunch* (1991) was a surreally accurate adaptation of William Burroughs' novel. A great deal of its self-contained universe comes from the unique musical application of Ornette Coleman blowing bebop jazz across Moroccan percussion rhythms. *M Butterfly* (1993) indulged their shared passion for opera. Then *Crash* (1996) was scored for six electric guitars, three harps, three winds and two percussionists. It's an ideal reaction to the auto-erotic and fetishistic story of car crash survivors. *eXistenZ* (1999) similarly played with instrumental make-up, though this time on a full orchestra's scale. It also played with the dynamics and acoustics of the recording room to musically reflect the fact you're never actually seeing what's really happening in the film until the very end.

Outside of the Cronenberg collaborations, Shore became the leading light for one of the few dubious trends that formed in the 90s. Quite why there have been so many serial killer movies is a troubling mystery. However, with *Silence Of The Lambs* (1991) a genre was born. Multiple Oscar nominations (although inexplicably not the score) showed this was held in higher regard than the 70s and 80s style of schlock horror. Shore's music has been cloned to death for subsequent movies that want to conjure foreboding and terror. In its original setting it's responsible for what was touted on its release to be the most frightening movie of all time. Take the pounding heartbeat of music away when 'Lecter Escapes' and the rapid cutting of people running about means nothing. Amazingly, Shore matched the dramatic intensity 4 years later with the mercilessly negative *Se7en*. After its enormously influential opening title sequence visuals, the score is relentlessly oppressive. Cold and insinuating, it conveys a constant threat from the killer's manipulating hand, and the dark, wet city that created him. For the desert finale, stabbing chords make the arrival of an innocuous delivery van seem like the most frightening event in the whole movie.

Before Shore returned to the genre in explosive style by utilising the dramatically non-Western sound of the Master Musicians Of Jajouka for *The Cell* (2000), and before Dr Lecter returned courtesy of Hans Zimmer in *Hannibal* (2001), the decade was filled with glossy glorifications of serial killers. Only a small list is needed to illustrate this: *Basic Instinct*, *Knight Moves*, *Dr Giggles* (all 1992), *Young Poisoner's Handbook*, *Copycat* (both 1995), *Kiss The Girls* (1997), *In Dreams*, *Fallen* (both 1998) and *The Bone Collector* (1999). Director John Waters is about the only person whose sense of humour could be forgiven for stretching to *Serial Mom* (1994), but humour did find its way into the horror genre with *I Know What You Did Last Summer* (1997) and *Urban Legend* (1998). Responsible for this shift was one of the 90s' biggest success stories, *Scream* (1996).

Postmodern irony is a term applied to a lot of film and TV in *Scream*'s wake. The first part of the idea is that characters are well versed in pop culture worlds and poke fun at them. The second part (the irony) is they don't know they're in a film or TV show straight out of one of those worlds. Marco Beltrami was the composer hired to write a score for *Scream* that fused old and new styles. It came about in several unique ways. "There was this radio show that interviewed me on the Internet, and (director) Wes Craven's assistant asked if they knew any composers they could recommend. I then had a meeting and they gave me the opening Drew Barrymore scene to score on spec." It was also a fairly unique situation in that Beltrami had never seen a horror film before! "Wes taught me a lot about how to maximise the scare potential in horror movies. One common rule is if nobody's there you sting it, and if the killer's there you go silent." Hence the musical red herring when Sydney opens an empty closet's door. Beltrami uses this technique in the rest of the trilogy, and also in his scores for *Mimic* (1997), *The Faculty* (1998) and *Halloween H20* (1998), for which he provided additional music. Fusing established styles with dance rhythms has been prevalent in horror and related genre movies ever since.

The other mainstream discoveries of the 90s came out of genre pictures too. Elliot Goldenthal had worked on a few earlier movies, but it was with *Alien³* (1992) that audience and industry ears pricked up with discomfort and intrigue. Before the film even starts, the composer messes with you through a torturously tailored re-recording of Alfred Newman's 20th Century-Fox Fanfare. "That was almost like knocking over Lenin's statue," Goldenthal recalls amusedly. "Digital recording came along, and we had 40 minutes of musicians' time at the end of the recording session. So rather than tell them to go plus pay them, Fox said they wanted a digital recording of the logo. Then I said: 'it's *Alien*. You think I can mess with it? Can I be subversive with it? So you're lulled into a state of non-comprehension.' We didn't have any score, so I just got up on the stand and told the musicians what to do on what note. It wasn't totally improvised. With ninety musicians, you have to be quite concise. You can't just say: 'try something here!' That's one hundred and eighty eyes looking attentively at you..." Within a short space of time, many more eyes were pointed his way, once his grinding, shrieking, yet often bitter-sweet style began getting Oscar nominations with *Interview With The Vampire* (1994). It's a style that's influenced plenty of scores in the same way as the fusion method. In fact, he was a pioneer of fusing styles pre-*Scream* himself, especially with the high-profile *Batman Forever* (1995).

London composer David Arnold was plucked from obscurity and given the sci-fi blockbuster *Stargate* (1994). Full of the romance rejuvenated by John Williams for *Star Wars* and sly nods to other popular soundtracks (listen for *633 Squadron* in the final battle), the score showed what happens when a soundtrack enthusiast is given a big break. It led to the enormous spoof and noise score of *Independence Day* (1996), which was as big as movies could be in the mid-90s. His next major project allowed him to reach back into his childhood and the reason he was in the industry at all. "When I saw *You Only Live Twice* (1967) as a lad, John Barry's music just took my head off completely. That was it. Bond to me is trying to keep it cool. Its metal-tip winkle-pickers. Loafers with steel toecaps. So when I did *Tomorrow Never Dies* (1997), it had to be done with all that in mind. I did talk to John up front about it, as someone I respect and admire. I didn't want to piss him off really. He said he thought I was the one person who could do it. That from the Guvnor! Then we went out and got drunk." The film and score resurrected the flagging spy series after a limp introduction for Pierce Brosnan in *Goldeneye* (1995), which had a decidedly non-Bondian musical accompaniment from Eric Serra. Arnold more than made amends with his homage to Barry crossed with drum and bass, and took things further for the rocking, sample-laced *The World Is Not Enough* (1999).

Could You Turn It Up?

If action movies and sample-driven scoring had a nursing home in the 90s, it was named Media Ventures Entertainment Group, LLC. In its infancy it was a one-room arrangement for Hans Zimmer and producer Jay Rifkin to work on *Rain Man* (1988). With the subsequent successes of *Black Rain*, *Days Of Thunder* (1990), *Pacific Heights* (1990) and specifically *Backdraft* (1991), he expanded the operation with a purpose-built facility in Santa Monica, where he invited other composers to house their studios. Zimmer's style of overlaying a massive orchestra with synthesiser effects (especially percussive) quickly spread to those working under the same roof. Many collaborative efforts resulted in multiple names credited on a score. Mark Mancina was one to spread his wings and go elsewhere after his *Speed* (1994) most definitely helped define the action movie score of the 90s. He then applied the style to the hits *Bad Boys* (1995) and *Twister* (1996). Other high-octane action extravaganzas produced within the MV complex include: *White Squall* (1996) by Jeff Rona for director Ridley Scott, *Face/Off* (1997) by John Powell for director John Woo, *Armageddon* (1998) by Trevor Rabin for director Michael Bay, and *Enemy Of The State* (1998) by Trevor Rabin and Harry Gregson-Williams for director Tony Scott.

Aside from the massive collaboration that resulted in multiple award glory for Disney's *The Lion King* (1994), their other popular pooling of resources was on *The Rock* (1996), which credits Nick Glennie-Smith,

Zimmer and Harry Gregson-Williams. Zimmer himself has continued to carry the action torch for *Crimson Tide* (1995), *Broken Arrow* (1996), *The Peacemaker* (1997), *Mission: Impossible 2* (2000) and *Gladiator* (2000). He explained his thinking behind the latter, "All the action sequences, the battles, came from sitting up to my ankles in mud in this tent which was like a palace with all these beautiful sculptures around me in gold. Ridley Scott explained that Marcus Aurelius fought this battle for something like 17 years and he would actually have these busts and art-work all around him. The thing that we love about the Roman civilisation is the elegance of the architecture and the art. All of it was at my feet, plus this blood-soaked earth. I had this crazy idea to find the most formal and beautiful musical form that I could think of which would reflect this beauty. I suddenly thought of Viennese waltzes, which are so happy and gay with a veneer of culture attached to them. So I made waltzes for the battle scenes which are incredibly savage." The cross-pollination of ideas and musical forms like these resulted in Zimmer's appointment as Head of Music when the Dreamworks SKG studio was founded in the mid-90s.

Several industry factors have influenced, affected and resulted from the MV scenario. Most pertinent is the final sound mix. "It's not hard to do right," claims Danny Elfman. "It's just hard the way things are done today. Films now are sonically such cluttered messes. Music and sound-effects people are all doing the same things for the same moments of film. The directors don't understand how to separate the two after the fact, so you get a little of both all the time. You get these cluttered monsters, which is about 85% to 90% of Hollywood movies today. The bigger the budget, it'll be a sonic catastrophe." A case in point would be *Armageddon*, where nearly every review made mention of the sheer volume of noise.

There are sadly many other examples of tampering or studio interfer-ence that have hindered the film composer's craft at the tail end of the 20th Century. The system is now highly reliant on the results of test screenings, where a random grouping of cinemagoers is empowered to tickbox aspects of a film into being changed. This often leads to reshoot-ing footage, which of course means musical edits or complete rescoring of scenes. Worse still, it can lead to what's known as a "tossed score" if too many voters consider the music unsupportive. Replacement scores, nearly always by a different composer, are something collectors increas-ingly despair at. There have been scattered instances of this in years gone by, like Ron Goodwin's score replacing Sir William Walton's on *Battle Of Britain*. Goodwin also replaced Henry Mancini on Hitchcock's *Frenzy*

(1972). Yet it got to the point during the 90s that withdrawing big name composers' work was commonplace. For example in 1998, Ennio Morricone was replaced by Michael Kamen for *What Dreams May Come*, and John Barry by John Ottman on *Goodbye Lover*.

One technological advancement that's proved damaging on many film scores is digital editing. Although a blessing for film-makers to work fast and meet release deadlines, it has played havoc with scores having to stay in constant flux up to the last minute as scenes change in length and sequence. One of the biggest victims of this was John Williams' *The Phantom Menace* (1999). After George Lucas had finished editing, Williams resequenced and added material to make a confusing album. It caused monumental fan outrage and so another CD was released the following year. Even that didn't pacify aficionados however, and neither in any way acknowledged the extent to which the music had been cut and pasted for the film.

Finding more than one album representing a movie is something buyers have had to muddle through for some time now. After *Batman* in 1989, Danny Elfman regularly suffered the indignity of having his music temporarily forgotten while song compilations filled shelves. There were three albums for *Dick Tracy*, then two for *Mission: Impossible*, *Men In Black*, and even for the inexplicable *Psycho* remake! Others already mentioned include: the *Scream* trilogy, *Batman Forever*, *Armageddon*, *Speed* and *Twister*. Those last two also carried the 'Inspired by' heading that's proven so misleading to collectors and casual buyers alike. The progression of things has happened over a very short space of time. In 1994, buyers were perfectly happy with *Pulp Fiction* mixing up dialogue and songs heard only fleetingly in the film. The two-CD set for *Forrest Gump* had songs heard even more fleetingly. Labels began to stop indicating which tracks were to be found in a film, leading to the 'From and inspired by' albums for *Batman And Robin* (1997) and *The Matrix* (1999) where you're left to guess. Countless more examples swamped the market in the latter half of the 90s, meaning film composers' work ended up being represented in several equally unsatisfactory ways: a token gesture of one or two tracks after a list of songs, or on a separate album held back so as not to impede sales of a preceding song compilation, or just not at all. The result of this is a complete loss of public understanding of what a soundtrack album is.

The only technological bright spot in the same time-frame was the emergence of Laser Disc and DVD, which allows for isolated music tracks and documentary explanations of a score. Naturally that's only of small recompense to the modern composer regularly affected by all the above.

Who's The Man?

The 90s started out well enough for the biggest of the names covered. For instance, John Barry bounced back from a bout of serious illness to win an Oscar for *Dances With Wolves* (1990). At that point it was still possible for him to conceive a score in his traditional way. "Kevin [Costner] showed me about 20 minutes of the opening, so I got a feeling of the texture of the movie. Then I went away and wrote 20 minutes of themes, knowing there had to be a 'John Dunbar Theme', knowing there had to be a journey theme when he takes off across this landscape. I never viewed *Dances With Wolves* as a Western but this very heroic story of a man getting on a horse and riding across America. Everything I wrote in that movie was through his eyes. I had to dramatically get inside him and put myself on that horse. I hate writing music where I'm outside like the camera." Barry got to apply his methodology to *Chaplin* (1992) and a couple more, but by the time of *The Specialist* (1994) he was being affected by market trends with his score album delayed so as not to affect sales of the song collection. Later in the decade there were numerous instances of Barry being replaced on a scoring assignment, including *The Horse Whisperer* (1998) and the aforementioned *Goodbye Lover*.

The triumvirate of A-list composers from the 70s and 80s (Williams, Goldsmith, Horner) had an interesting decade to say the least, each in their own way demonstrating the state of the industry. John Williams remained the most Oscar-nominated person alive largely thanks to the continued collaboration with Steven Spielberg. *Schindler's List* was the award winner over *Jurassic Park* when both arrived in 1993. Aside from multiple nominations for deserving works like *JFK* (1991) and *Saving Private Ryan* (1998), it was otherwise a pretty lean decade for the composer after the massive successes of the 70s and 80s.

Jerry Goldsmith began the 90s in true style with what many consider to be his last great action score for *Total Recall* (1990). At the time he announced it would be the last of its type he would do, referring to the densely complex orchestrations for the large number of action set pieces. One of many examples of Goldsmith's great skill is a sequence of Schwarzenegger being told he's acting out a dream inside his head, where the dialogue turns into an explosive fight. For this the music blends a piccolo with electronics, creating an ambiguous texture leaving the audience unable to interpret the dialogue as reality or fantasy. For the fight there are rapidly overlapping rhythms to keep up with Paul Verhoeven's breathless directorial style. They reunited for *Basic Instinct* (1992) with a main title that ebbs and flows with sensuality that was one of the most emulated pieces for several years. He managed to keep up the promise of avoiding action material for the early part of the decade with a few romances and comedies like *The Russia House* (1990), *Love Field* (1992), *Rudy* (1993) and *Angie* (1994). Then that promise seemed to be completely forgotten. There followed: *The Shadow* (1994), *First Knight* (1995), *Chain Reaction* and *Executive Decision* (both 1996), *Air Force One* (1997), *U.S. Marshals* (1998), *The Haunting*, *The 13th Warrior* and *The Mummy* (all 1999), and a reunion with Verhoeven once more for *Hollow Man* (2000). With many similar in between (e.g. the two *Star Treks*), it seemed Goldsmith was enslaved to the Hollywood action machine. His own personality pervades these powerhouse pieces, but at nowhere near the inventive level of the decades before. It is merely a reflection of the films themselves of course. Yet even the one critical highlight of the period, *L.A. Confidential* (1997), is little more than an amalgam of his earlier *Chinatown* and the action material developed in these others.

L.A. Confidential stood no chance in the Oscar race that year of course. The juggernaut of *Titanic* could not be stopped, and James Horner's unprecedented album sales had to be acknowledged. Critical (and the collecting community's) opinion about period anachronisms, startling similarities to Enya's song 'Book Of Days', and love/hate for Celine Dion's voice are all rather immaterial ultimately. "I wanted to write a score that was deeply emotional," he explained. "I had to choose a palette of colours that would do that for me. My Irish guys and Sissel Kyrkjebø because they're so intimate. Jim [Cameron, the director] wanted desperately not to have a big Hollywood extravaganza score that they've put on a thousand other films. They all sound the same no matter who writes them. By the same token, although the film takes place in 1912 I didn't want to write some precious little English chamber piece that would narrate the period. It had to be some timeless fusion. I was looking for colours that weren't conventional ways to sell a period film. I wanted to feel what I might have felt had I been on board and lost something very dear to me. The sinking didn't really matter. It takes care of itself in the watching. It didn't really matter what music I put to it, it's already so spectacular. What I felt needed my help more was the depth of passion between them. The profound loss that Rose feels. The way the story turns itself around at the end and goes full circle. All those sort of wistful mystical feelings I wanted to convey in the music." Horner's thinking answers many criticisms, and the influence on the industry whereby composers now either aim straight for or run far away from uilleann pipes answers many more. To put *Titanic* into context for the composer's own decade, it should be noted that the Irish elements (whistle and bhodrán drums) followed in the footsteps of his *Patriot Games* (1992), *Legends Of The Fall* (1994), *Braveheart* (1995) and *The Devil's Own* (1997). Thematically the material owed much to his *Thunderheart* (1992), *Bopha!* (1993), *Courage Under Fire* (1996) and others. Like Goldsmith, it's felt his last truly inspired works came at the beginning of the 90s. Namely the charm of *The Rocketeer* (1991) with its 30s innocence and serial adventure conveyed in a joyous flying theme, and *Sneakers* (1992) with its bluesy team motif and subtle suspense underscore.

There's Too Many Of Them

Of the director/composer relationships that blossomed in the 80s, several bore influential fruit. Eric Serra's *Leon* (1994) for Luc Besson solidified an electronic palette of sounds and a style that won him the next James Bond movie (*Goldeneye*). Other composers have attempted that sound a lot. Later with *The Fifth Element* (1997), they took that style much further, memorably for a dazzling display of electronically manipulated opera singing. Angelo Badalamenti worked with David Lynch for a couple more aurally sumptuous pieces. Firstly with fellow composer Barry Adamson on *Lost Highway* (1996) with its uniquely appropriate selection of needle-dropped songs (meaning fragmentary extracts). Then *The Straight Story* (1999) was a surprise departure from dark surrealism. Instead the life-affirming tale features a blend of Country and Americana guaranteed to result in not a dry eye in the house. At the opposite end of the emotional scale was Patrick Doyle's gothic horror for *Mary Shelley's Frankenstein* (1994) with Kenneth Branagh. Away from the Shakespearean adaptations, Doyle let rip with a blisteringly furious orchestra, especially for 'The Creation' scene and its 2 minutes of all-out sensory assault.

Outside the security of the composer A-list and working partnerships, the 90s were sprinkled with individual highlights. There were more composers working and more albums being released than ever before. In chronological order, here are some of the moments of note...

Ghost (1990) remains one of the best examples of a song selling an album. Alex North's 'Unchained Melody,' as interpreted by the Righteous Brothers, kept the album in US charts for over a year. The record label Varèse Sarabande was by this point establishing itself as the foremost soundtrack producer, and the success of their score album for Maurice Jarre meant they stayed leader of the pack. A year later, director Nicholas Meyer tried to repeat his trick of a decade earlier (when he launched James Horner's career on *Star Trek II*) by giving Cliff Eidelman his big break on *Star Trek VI: The Undiscovered Country*. Meyer's classical roots shone through in elements fashioned after Holst and Stravinsky, but the young composer's Golden Age take on the franchise unfortunately didn't carve him as big a name as for Horner.

An element of confusion surrounded the names on *The Last Of The Mohicans* (1992) with a screencard putting a double space between Trevor Jones and Randy Edelman. Only record buyers would discover who was responsible for the majestically soaring hero music, and who for the ambient synthesiser inserts. That same year, there was no uncertainty that Polish composer Wojciech Kilar was solely responsible for the hypnotic grimness of *Bram Stoker's Dracula*. His middle-European style clashed welcomely with Hollywood's. No one else would have scored the hearse chase finale with an insanely repetitive scherzo (vigorous movement of music).

In 1994, Michael Nyman's *The Piano* sold over 3 million copies worldwide, and remains his most popular work. *The Usual Suspects* (1995) remains newcomer John Ottman's most popular too, with its film noir tone and rhythmic perfection derived from the fact he was also the film's editor. It took a trio of composers to keep up with the editing and romance of *Romeo + Juliet* (1996), but the orchestral/contemporary electronics/song fusion from Craig Armstrong, Nelle Hooper and Marius De Vries has been much emulated (particularly Armstrong's choral elements). Far subtler and tender expressiveness was required for romance and the love that dare not speak its name in *Wilde* (1997). The emotive score from British composer Debbie Wiseman declared both the scribe's genius and its own.

Right at the dawn of the new Millennium came three potentially trend-setting scores in an otherwise lacklustre 1999. First were Jon Brion's unusually long cues linking the many disparate threads of *Magnolia* together. Then in amongst sourced drum and bass (e.g. The Propellerheads 'Spybreak' which was promptly reused or mimicked to death) for *The Matrix* is a sassy blend of atonal brass fanfare and techno from Don Davis. Lastly there was *Fight Club* with a kitchen sink collection of every conceivable method of scoring applied by The Dust Brothers. Into the new century, *Crouching Tiger Hidden Dragon* by Chinese composer Tan Dun would prove to be the most memorable new soundtrack experience. In an even more lacklustre year, it was without doubt the most deserving of Oscar gold.

The extended Newman family warrant mention. Thomas seems to have a split musical personality, dividing himself between the uplifting symphonic style of *The Shawshank Redemption* (1994) and the pots and pans electronics of *American Beauty* (1999). Randy excels as a song-writer, yet is just as at home warming every sportingly patriotic American's heart for *The Natural* (1984) or recalling the child in everyone for *Toy Story* (1995). David is a well-respected conductor who always seems to be most at home with slapstick comedy like *Bill And Ted's Excellent Adventure* (1988) or *Galaxy Quest* (1999). Another name to gain prominence through the 90s was James Newton Howard. His subtly supportive work with director M. Night Shyamalan on the mysteries of *The Sixth Sense* (1999) and *Unbreakable* (2000) looks set to forge another great director/composer relationship.

You'll have noted repeat mention of the Hollywood A-list toward the end of this chronology. Apart from financially motivated lists in places like The Hollywood Reporter, it's rare anyone cares to name names. Suffice to say, this last chapter just has.

A Final Thought

What does all this winding down and miscellany mean? Where film scoring is concerned, too many cooks have most definitely spoiled the broth. Working in this last decade were an enormous number of composers, yet so few fall within the important criteria of influencing the industry. As promised at the start of the book, the names have gone by pretty fast, therefore many have had to slip through the cracks of the 90s like: John Debney, Carter Burwell, Bruce Broughton, Mychael Danna, Randy Edelman, George Fenton, Mark Isham, Joel McNeely, Rachel Portman, Graeme Revell, Marc Shaiman, Stephen Warbeck and Gabriel Yared. Also those whose careers originated before the 90s: Luis Bacalov, Richard Rodney Bennett, John Corigliano, Carl Davis, Brad Fiedel, Ernest

Gold, John Green, Quincy Jones, Stanley Myers, Mario Nascimbene, Jean-Claude Petit, Nicola Piovani, Zbigniew Preisner, André Prévin, Richard Robbins, Philippe Sarde and John Scott. To them and their fans, as well as to many others (particularly international composers), this book apologises for their absence.

It really isn't all doom and gloom by any means. History repeats itself nowadays more than it ever used to. The industry's future is therefore sure to enjoy an unexpected surprise or two. Whether you were a film music geek fan before reading this book or not, rest assured there'll always be plenty to make listening to the screen worth your while.

7. Hitting The Right Note

This is a condensed step-by-step look at the craft of scoring a modern film.

1) The point at which a composer comes aboard is dependent on many of the factors highlighted in Chapter 6. If they have a working relationship with a director, it's not uncommon to visit the set while filming. In general, a composer will be approached toward the end of shooting to check they're available. Concurrent to this, a music editor compiles a temp track of existing music to work with early edits of the film.

2) The very first thing a composer is given is either a script or rough cut of footage to view. Danny Elfman explains his preference, "I need an assembly. A script doesn't do anything for me at all. Any time I've tried to jump the gun and get musical ideas from a script, I've ended up scrapping them all. You can shoot a script a hundred different ways. What works for me best is to come into the first rough assembly with an absolutely blank slate, no preconceived ideas at all. First impressions are very important, which is why I need my tape recorder to hand. In fact, very often I tell the director not to be alarmed if I run out. I'll get ideas and literally take my recorder and charge down to the lobby."

3) Next comes a repeat viewing with the director (and sometimes the producers) with the specific purpose of 'spotting' the film. This is a process of identifying where music cues should begin and end. Here the music editor helps the composer determine cue lengths and keep abreast of any changes.

4) With a number of 'starts' in mind, it all comes down to the blank score page and being sat at the piano/keyboard. "Inspiration is a very difficult thing to talk about," states John Williams. "Sometimes you feel the flow, and sometimes you don't. The results don't always correspond to the way we feel. The things we do that we think are the highest from an inspirational point of view are not. The things we dash off on the way to work in a taxi might dig deeper or reach higher."

Inspiration is one thing, but where do you start? "Personally, finding the musical hook that will be the central core of the theme is the most important part of the initial composition process," says Debbie Wiseman. "Somehow, when the key theme is in place, all else follows quite naturally. This key musical idea can happen almost immediately, or else it can take an age to materialise. It's simply a case of keeping going until it happens."

Composers like Williams and Wiseman put pencil to paper to sketch out ideas. With so much technology to play with, composers can have many different approaches to composition. Hans Zimmer explains his: "Having had no musical education whatsoever other than piano lessons for 2 weeks, which if anything damaged my way forward because they never taught me anything, I use a Macintosh. I use sequencing software, then some samplers which basically have a fake orchestra in them."

5) Once the ideas are flowing, it's quite usual for a series of electronic demos or 'mock-ups' to be requested from the composer to accompany the scenes being edited. Then it becomes a race against time to meet a pre-booked recording session date. "Just to get two minutes of orchestral music a day on paper is really hard," reveals Danny Elfman. "Everyone has their own system of working. I put it up on a big board. I break down the number of cues into their minutes and seconds. I total it knowing I can write roughly two minutes a day. I have a countdown of days at the top, and there's a certain point, a D-Day, where I must write two minutes a day to make it to the end on time. I'm always watching that point coming, and I'll try to do my development knowing that freight train is coming. But it's inconceivable to ever not be finished in time."

6) Time being of the essence, a composer will often work with one or more orchestrators to lessen the load. Elfman has been working with Steve Bartek ever since they played in the band Oingo Boingo together. Here is Bartek's definition of the job: "The role of the orchestrator in film music is multifaceted, involving some creativity, technique and organisation. First and foremost I'm responsible for translating a composer's sketch into an orchestral (ensemble) piece of music that sounds just as they envisioned it. I make sure it is as easily playable by the musicians as possible so as not to waste any time on the scoring stage. I often make sure it fits the dramatic and stylistic concerns of the scene, that the music is large enough for the action or small enough for the dialogue, and that the instrument choices are appropriate for the scene. I'm also involved in the management of resources to produce the music. Acting as the liaison between composer and the orchestra contractor I ensure the needed musicians are at the right session at the right time for the most efficient way to get the music recorded. This involves having an organised recording order that will save money on musicians and make it easier for them and the engineer to move quickly from one cue to the next by keeping similar recording set-ups and music styles next to each other. I'm often called upon by the music editor to facilitate any last-minute movie changes by editing the music to fit any new version of the scene. I'm usually at the

sessions making sure it all happens as smoothly as possible, helping make any corrections or changes called for by the composer or director while musicians are on the stand. Of course when something goes wrong it's always the orchestrator's fault, as it should be."

7) Bartek's intermediate administrative decisions ensure a recording venue is settled on, and the number of sessions needed are determined by the amount of music to be recorded. The players themselves are booked by an orchestra contractor depending on how many have been orchestrated for and who's available. In Los Angeles there is a large selection of session players, whereas the UK often makes use of several long-standing orchestras (e.g. the LSO).

With everything in place, the individual pages for players to follow must be created. The full score is given to a copyist either in handwritten A3 format or as a computer file. They then transcribe for each instrumentalist bearing several points in mind. The parts have to show the number of bars to rest, otherwise a player is looking at empty space and rustling unnecessary pages. The page turns need to be when the player has a free hand. For neatness and speed, this is generally all fed into a piece of software such as Sibelius 7.

8) The set-up of a recording studio is extremely important given the amounts of money often involved. Dick Lewzey has worked for many years at London's CTS Studios. He broke down the stages of set-up and his role as recording engineer like this: "A composer calls to ask you aboard first of all. A venue is considered based on the size of orchestra and the sort of sound they want. Is it to be an acoustic recording or something really in-your-face? You're usually booked for the room a day in advance of the session. The music editor comes in with click track machines (which play the instrumentalists' beats for them to follow in their headphones) and they test the video machines and talkback (a simple two-way communication from control room to conductor podium). Then there may be a two-man team putting out microphones, cables and headphones. Sometimes it's just me. The time this takes depends on the room and number of players. A recent one hundred and fifty-piece orchestra with choir took nearly 6 hours to set up. It was 7:00pm to 2:00am. Usually it's around 3 to 4 hours. I never delegate microphone placement to anyone else though. I allocate mikes to certain tracks on the tape machine. Sometimes they want to separate soloists to give the option of cutting them out later. When we start the session, I have to achieve a headphone balance for the players, and then tweak as we go. One of the hardest things is monitoring click track noise doesn't spill out of head-

phones during quiet passages. Another job during the session is going into the studio and talking to players. With percussion you have to talk about where to stand to catch everything for the way you've set up. During the actual takes I try to catch every cue on their own merits. Beyond this I have to ensure the people who are mixing at the dubbing session know what they're getting on the tapes. Then afterwards there's the clean-up. An eighty-piece orchestra can devastate a room. There's spilled tea on cables and cups everywhere!"

9) Of all the aspects of putting a modern score together, conducting is the one where opinion's most divided. The A-list triumvirate of John Williams, Jerry Goldsmith and James Horner all conduct their own work, as do John Barry and Debbie Wiseman. Others such as David Arnold, Danny Elfman and Hans Zimmer do not, feeling it is more important to be in the recording booth to be hands-on for any changes requested by the director or producers. For the case in favour, here's what Howard Shore has to say: "I think that conducting is a way to fully realise your music. It's the final stage in a way. From the podium you can offer so much expression and advice to the players you can't do from the control room. There are many things you can quickly do from the podium with your players, from marking score parts to talking about phrasing, dynamics, interpretation, to changing a melody line slightly with grace notes. Film music is done quickly. It's not like you can finish a score and have a month to go over every small detail. From the podium you can work with the orchestration and hear these balances and assess the performance of the players first-hand. It's all about getting a great performance on tape essentially. The essence of it is really about rehearsal, because the players have never seen it. You want to take them through the rehearsal process as quickly as possible. Then when the energy is correct, do the best take. Quite often the best film takes are early ones. So there's a fantastic immediacy of being on the podium and feeling the energy of the players when you're going to get that great take. You can see if they're getting a little tired, or maybe it's getting a little near lunch, or maybe we need to take a break. It's somewhat about control. There's no chain of command."

10) The recordings are mixed in two stages. Each cue can have instrument volumes tinkered with to achieve desired effects. A full balance is achieved, and it's also the time an album is put together. Then comes the final 'dub,' where composers fear to tread. The final sound mix for the film is where the music's function in the film is set. Many modern scores are thought lost in high volumes of dialogue and Foley (replacement

sound effects). For film music, this is where the buck either stops or is made.

11) There can be no one more qualified to comment on album production than Robert Townson, who has worked on over five hundred soundtracks. "The sequence of events that ultimately lead to a finished soundtrack can vary wildly. More often than not these days, it seems the production work on a soundtrack CD ends up pushed to the last possible moment. Composers are writing and recording music until as little as a month before the film opens. There are composers and studios I work with more frequently than others. Under these circumstances, however, even if I may know I'll be releasing the next Jerry Goldsmith score in advance, there's not much you can do until there is music to work with. Beginning either during the recording of the score or immediately following its completion, I will work with the composer to determine which cues from the score best lend themselves to be included on the soundtrack. At this stage we may have union restrictions that limit the amount of music we are able to include. If not, these decisions can be purely artistic in nature, where our goal can solely be to make the best CD possible from all the music recorded. Once most of these decisions are made, I will arrange for a mastering session where, with the aid of a mastering engineer, we assemble the score in its album sequence. This can be a thrilling event since this is the first time you hear the listening experience of what will be the final CD. Following this, after receiving a reference disc or first draft of the CD, we are able to make changes to the sequence, adjust the spacing between cuts, fine-tune the sound with additional EQ adjustments and then, finally, arrive at a finished master. Once the music's locked it becomes a race to complete the packaging. Cue titles, album credits, artwork and photos from the studio and the film's billing block must all be assembled in a hopefully artistic way. There can be any number of roadblocks along the way. Delays or denials for songs from other labels intended for inclusion, last-minute changes in the key art… you name it. There have even been a few rare but tragic occasions where the score ends up being tossed out of the picture after we've already completed the CD! When things go smoothly, however, all of the work is done so quickly that you can barely remember doing it once you are all through. In no time at all I'm on to the next one."

8. Reference

Books On Composers

There's a shockingly small library on the lives of film composers. Long-promised works expected soon include a look at the Newman family and a biography of John Williams. Nearly everything released has gone out of print (but try through the magazines listed below), hence this paltry list of two:

John Barry: A Life In Music by Geoff Leonard, Pete Walker & Gareth Bramley, Hardback, 243 pages, 1998, Sansom & Company, ISBN 1-900178-86-9 - If ever there was a labour of love, this is it. Bulging with information and colour photographs, this is the way all great film composers deserve to be represented.

A Heart At Fire's Centre (The Life And Music Of Bernard Herrmann) by Steven C Smith, Hardback, 415 pages, 1991, University Of California Press, ISBN 0-520-07123-9 - A truly masterful work on the life of a composer. Covers his private life, film career and concert works with equal respect and detail.

General Books On Film Music

Again there's not much of a library available, and much of what is can often get quite academic. I've left out those that are aimed toward the musicians themselves. These offer a nice cross-section of areas of the industry:

Music For The Movies by Tony Thomas, Paperback, 330 pages, 1997, Silman-James Press, ISBN 1-879505-37-1 - Originally printed in 1971, it focuses on the Golden and Silver Ages. This was the first (and still the best) book to tackle the subject.

musicHound Soundtracks, edited by Didier C Deutsch, Paperback, 872 pages, 2000, Visible Ink Press, ISBN 1-57859-101-5 - An invaluable oversized compilation of album reviews currently available.

The Score by Michael Schelle, Paperback, 427 pages, 1999, Silman-James Press, ISBN 1-879505-40-1 - Fifteen composer interviews by a fellow composer. Lots of interesting anecdotes, but inevitably gets quite technical at times.

Screencraft: Film Music by Mark Russell & James Young, Paperback, 192 pages, 2000, RotoVision, ISBN 2-88046-441-2 - Similar to *The Score*, but its thirteen interviews are far shorter and less insightful. Don't be fooled by large format; there's not much in it.

Sound And Vision by Jon Burlingame, Paperback, 244 pages, 2000, Billboard Books, ISBN 0823084272 - Following a fact-filled history of film music recordings is an equally informative spotlight on the most important albums, sorted by composer.

Specialist Magazines

Printing advancements have allowed fanzines to move away from the photocopier. While there is plenty of fannish debate and opinion about, the ones with the most to say are below. Their website URLs are given since up-to-the-minute news will be there first.

Film Score Monthly – www.filmscoremonthly.com - Possessed of a singular sardonic wit, it may not be as regular as its title suggests, but it's glossily attractive and informative. The Los Angeles editorial team are also responsible for a terrific ongoing series of classic soundtrack albums.

Music From The Movies – www.musicfromthemovies.com/ - With an enormous album reviews section, and feature articles of biblical proportions, this UK-based magazine has gone from strength to strength. Website is home to the international Film Music Critics Jury.

Soundtrack – www.soundtrackmag.com/ - Printed in Belgium, this is a slightly smaller-sized variant of *Music From The Movies*, but with a refreshing leaning toward European works.

Internet Resources

The soundtrack community is nowhere more alive than on the Internet. Newsgroups and private lists chronicle excitement and dismay at new titles with either alarming or amusing degrees of fervour. Some of the sites listed here contain their own chat forums, but log into rec.music.movies some time and enjoy the noise!

Review

Album review sites are plentiful on the Web. The better ones also feature articles and interviews:

Cinemusic – www.cinemusic.net/
Film Music On The Web – musicweb.vavo.com/film/index.htm
Film Tracks – www.filmtracks.com/
Movie Music UK – www.shef.ac.uk/~cm1jwb/mmuk.htm
Movie Tunes – www.hollywood.com/movietunes/
Moviewave – www.moviewave.freeserve.co.uk/
Score Logue – www.scorelogue.com/main.html
Score Reviews – www.scorereviews.com/
SoundtrackNet – www.soundtrack.net/
Tracksounds – www.tracksounds.com/

Appreciation

Fan sites appear and disappear regularly. Here's a mixture of official and unauthorised sites which seem to be around to stay:

David Arnold – www.davidarnold007.freeserve.co.uk/arnold.htm
John Barry – www.geocities.com/Hollywood/Bungalow/2802/jbarry.htm
Elmer Bernstein – www.elmerbernstein.com/
Danny Elfman – elfman.filmmusic.com/
Bernard Herrmann – www.uib.no/herrmann/
James Horner – www.hornershrine.com
Erich Wolfgang Korngold – korngold.freeyellow.com/
Ennio Morricone – www.enniomorricone.net/
Basil Poledouris – www.basilpoledouris.com/index88.html
Miklós Rózsa – www.freespeech.org/eclectica/miklos/index.html
Max Steiner – hometown.aol.com/steinerlib/index.htm
John Williams – www.classicalrecordings.com/johnwilliams
Franz Waxman – www.franzwaxman.com/main.html

Debbie Wiseman – www.debbiewiseman.co.uk/
Hans Zimmer – www.mediaventures.com/htmls/zimmer_b.html

Retail

Amazon (.com or .co.uk) is always a good bet for soundtracks. But here are a couple of specialists:

Intrada (San Francisco) – www.intrada.com/
Footlight Records (New York) – www.footlight.com/
Movie Boulevard (UK) – www.movieboulevard.co.uk

How To Build A CD Library

Since there are thousands of CDs available, and this book has touched on so many titles, here is a rough guide for a beginner's library. These fifty albums are listed in order of release, not priority or preference (of course by inclusion they betray a little of my own preference!) It should be noted that back-catalogue albums are deleted with alarming regularity now. Many compilation albums began appearing in the late 90s, so it's possible to acquire some of the classic themes that way. Most scores deserve complete presentation though, so the first part of the list covers those.

1933, *King Kong*, Max Steiner, Marco Polo 8223763
1935, *The Bride Of Frankenstein*, Franz Waxman, Silva Screen FILMCD 135
1938, *Alexander Nevsky*, Sergei Prokofiev, RCA Victor 09026-61926-2
1939, *Gone With The Wind*, Max Steiner, Rhino 72269
1941, *Citizen Kane*, Bernard Herrmann, Varèse Sarabande VSD-5806
1947, *The Ghost And Mrs Muir*, Bernard Herrmann, Varèse Sarabande VSD-5850
1951, *A Streetcar Named Desire*, Alex North, Varèse Sarabande VSD-5500
1958, *Vertigo*, Bernard Herrmann, Varèse Sarabande VSD-5759 (original) or 5600 (re-recording)
1959, *Ben-Hur*, Miklós Rózsa, Rhino 72197
1960, *Psycho*, Bernard Herrmann, Varèse Sarabande VSD-5765
1960, *The Magnificent Seven*, Elmer Bernstein, Rykodisc RCD 10741
1960, *Spartacus*, Alex North, MCA MCAD-10256
1964, *The Pink Panther*, Henry Mancini, BMG/Buddha Records 7446 5997252

1966, *The Good, The Bad, And The Ugly*, Ennio Morricone, EMI-Manhattan CDP 48408 2

1968, *Bullitt*, Lalo Schifrin, Warner Bros. 9362-45008-2

1968, *Planet Of The Apes*, Jerry Goldsmith, Varèse Sarabande VSD-5848

1975, *Jaws*, John Williams, Decca 467 045-2

1976, *Taxi Driver*, Bernard Herrmann, Arista 07822-19005-2

1977, *Star Wars/The Empire Strikes Back* (1980), John Williams, RCA Victor 09026 68746-2/68747-2 (Special Editions – I cheated here by putting both together!)

1978, *Superman*, John Williams, Warner Archives/Rhino R2 75874

1979, *Star Trek: The Motion Picture*, Jerry Goldsmith, Columbia/Legacy C2K 66134

1981, *Raiders Of The Lost Ark*, John Williams, Silva Screen Raiders 001

1982, *Blade Runner*, Vangelis, East West 4509-96574-2

1982, *Star Trek II: The Wrath Of Khan*, James Horner, GNP Crescendo GNPD 8022

1982, *Conan The Barbarian*, Basil Poledouris, Varèse Sarabande VSD-5390

1990, *Total Recall: The Deluxe Edition*, Jerry Goldsmith, Varèse Sarabande VSD-6197

1991, *Silence Of The Lambs*, Howard Shore, MCA MCAD-10194

1992, *The Last Of The Mohicans*, Trevor Jones & Randy Edelman, Varèse Sarabande VSD-6161

1992, *Bram Stoker's Dracula*, Wojciech Kilar, Columbia CK 53165

1995, *The Usual Suspects*, John Ottman, Milan 74321 30107-2

1996, *Lost Highway*, Angelo Badalamenti/Barry Adamson, Nothing/Interscope/MCA IND-90090

1996, *Scream*, Marco Beltrami, Varèse Sarabande VSD-5959 (with *Scream 2*)

1997, *Wilde*, Debbie Wiseman, MCI MPRCD-001

1999, *The World Is Not Enough*, David Arnold, Radioactive CD1121612

2000, *Crouching Tiger Hidden Dragon*, Tan Dun, Sony Classical SK 89347

Movie Collections

1996, *The Alien Trilogy*, Goldsmith/Horner/Goldenthal, Varèse Sarabande VSD-5753

1997, *The Batman Trilogy*, Elfman/Goldenthal/Hefti, Varèse Sarabande VSD-5766

1998, *The Hammer Film Music Collection Volume One*, Various, GDI Records GDICD002

1999, *Bond Back In Action* and *2* (2000), Various, Silva Screen FILMCD 317/340 (these for score)

1999, *The Best Of Bond... James Bond 007*, Various, Capitol Records CD BOND 99 (this for songs)

2000, *Fellini/Rota: La Dolce Vita*, Silva Screen FILMCD 720

2000, *A History Of Horror*, Various, Silva Screen FILMXCD 331

2001, *The Godfather Trilogy*, Rota/Coppola/Mascagni, Silva Screen FILMCD 344

Composer Collections

1990, *Music For A Darkened Theatre Volumes One* and *Two* (1996), Elfman, MCA MCAD-10065/MCAD2-11550 (again I cheated here by adding the two together)

1996, *Erich Wolfgang Korngold: The Warner Brothers Years*, Premiere Soundtracks 7243 8 38118 2 3

1998, *Titanic: The Essential James Horner Film Music Collection*, Silva Screen FILMXCD 197

1998, *The Omen: The Essential Jerry Goldsmith Film Music Collection*, Silva Screen FILMXCD 199

2000, *The Essential Maurice Jarre Film Music Collection*, Silva Screen FILMXCD 324

2000, *Ben-Hur: The Essential Miklós Rózsa Film Music Collection*, Silva Screen FILMXCD 334

2001, *John Barry: The Collection*, Silva Screen FILMXCD 349

The Essential Library

Build up your library with new titles every month

Alfred Hitchcock by Paul Duncan

More than 20 years after his death, Alfred Hithcock is still a household name, most people in the Western world have seen at least one of his films, and he popularised the action movie format we see every week on the cinema screen. He was both a great artist and dynamite at the box office. This book examines the genius and enduring popularity of one of the most influential figures in the history of the cinema!

Stanley Kubrick by Paul Duncan

Kubrick's work, like all masterpieces, has a timeless quality. His vision is so complete, the detail so meticulous, that you believe you are in a three-dimensional space displayed on a two-dimensional screen. He was commercially successful because he embraced traditional genres like War (*Paths Of Glory, Full Metal Jacket*), Crime (*The Killing*), Science Fiction (*2001*), Horror (*The Shining*) and Love (*Barry Lyndon*). At the same time, he stretched the boundaries of film with controversial themes: underage sex (*Lolita*); ultra violence (*A Clockwork Orange*); and erotica (*Eyes Wide Shut*).

Orson Welles by Martin Fitzgerald

The popular myth is that after the artistic success of *Citizen Kane* it all went downhill from there for Orson Welles, that he was some kind of fallen genius. Yet, despite overwhelming odds, he went on to make great Films Noirs like *The Lady From Shanghai* and *Touch Of Evil*. He translated Shakespeare's work into films with heart and soul (*Othello, Chimes At Midnight, Macbeth*), and he refused to take the bite out of modern literature, giving voice to bitterness, regret and desperation in *The Magnificent Ambersons* and *The Trial*. Far from being down and out, Welles became one of the first cutting-edge independent filmmakers.

Film Noir by Paul Duncan

The laconic private eye, the corrupt cop, the heist that goes wrong, the femme fatale with the rich husband and the dim lover - these are the trademark characters of Film Noir. This book charts the progression of the Noir style as a vehicle for film-makers who wanted to record the darkness at the heart of American society as it emerged from World War to the Cold War. As well as an introduction explaining the origins of Film Noir, seven films are examined in detail and an exhaustive list of over 500 Films Noirs are listed.

The Essential Library

Build up your library with new titles every month

Film Directors:

Jane Campion (£2.99)

Jackie Chan (£2.99)

David Cronenberg (£3.99)

Alfred Hitchcock (£3.99)

Stanley Kubrick (£2.99)

David Lynch (£3.99)

Sam Peckinpah (£2.99)

Orson Welles (£2.99)

Steven Spielberg (£3.99)

John Carpenter (£3.99)

Joel & Ethan Coen (£3.99)

Terry Gilliam (£2.99)

Krzysztof Kieslowski (£2.99)

Sergio Leone (£3.99)

Brian De Palma (£2.99)

Ridley Scott (£3.99)

Billy Wilder (£3.99)

Film Genres:

Film Noir (£3.99)

Horror Films (£3.99)

Spaghetti Westerns (£3.99)

Blaxploitation Films (£3.99)

Hong Kong Heroic Bloodshed (£2.99)

Slasher Movies(£3.99)

Vampire Films (£2.99)

Film Subjects:

Laurel & Hardy (£3.99)

Steve McQueen (£2.99)

The Oscars® (£3.99)

Bruce Lee (£3.99)

Marx Brothers (£3.99)

Marilyn Monroe (£3.99)

Filming On A Microbudget (£3.99)

TV:

Doctor Who (£3.99)

Literature:

Cyberpunk (£3.99)

Hitchhiker's Guide (£3.99)

Terry Pratchett (£3.99)

Philip K Dick (£3.99)

Noir Fiction (£2.99)

Sherlock Holmes (£3.99)

Ideas:

Conspiracy Theories (£3.99)

Feminism (£3.99)

Nietzsche (£3.99)

History:

Alchemy & Alchemists (£3.99)

The Crusades (£3.99)

Available at all good bookstores, or send a cheque to: **Pocket Essentials (Dept FM), 18 Coleswood Rd, Harpenden, Herts, AL5 1EQ, UK.** Please make cheques payable to 'Oldcastle Books.' Add 50p postage & packing for each book in the UK and £1 elsewhere.

US customers can send $6.95 plus $1.95 postage & packing for each book to: **Trafalgar Square Publishing, PO Box 257, Howe Hill Road, North Pomfret, Vermont 05053, USA.** e-mail: tsquare@sover.net

Customers worldwide can order online at **www.pocketessentials.com**.

The Essential Library

Build up your library with new titles every month

Tim Burton by Colin Odell & Michelle Le Blanc, £3.99

Tim Burton makes films about outsiders on the periphery of society. His heroes are psychologically scarred, perpetually naive and childlike, misunderstood or unintentionally disruptive. They upset convential society and morality. Even his villains are rarely without merit - circumstance blurs the divide between moral fortitude and personal action. But most of all, his films have an aura of the fairytale, the fantastical and the magical.

Film Music by Paul Tonks, £3.99

From *Ben-Hur* to *Star Wars* and *Psycho* to *Scream*, film music has played an essential role in such genre-defining classics. Making us laugh, cry, and jump with fright, it's the manipulative tool directors cannot do without. The turbulent history, the ever-changing craft, the reclusive or limelight-loving superstars, the enthusiastic world of fandom surrounding it, and the best way to build a collection, is all streamlined into a user-friendly guide for buffs and novices alike.

Woody Allen (Revised & Updated Edition) by Martin Fitzgerald, £3.99

Woody Allen: Neurotic. Jewish. Funny. Inept. Loser. A man with problems. Or so you would think from the characters he plays in his movies. But hold on. Allen has written and directed 30 films. He may be a funny man, but he is also one of the most serious American film-makers of his generation. This revised and updated edition includes *Sweet And Lowdown* and *Small Time Crooks*.

American Civil War by Phil Davies, £3.99

The American Civil War, fought between North and South in the years 1861-1865, was the bloodiest and most traumatic war in American history. Rival visions of the future of the United States faced one another across the battlefields and, as in any civil war, families and friends were bitterly divided by the conflict. Phil Davies looks at the deep-rooted causes of the war, so much more complicated than the simple issue of slavery.

American Indian Wars by Howard Hughes, £3.99

At the beginning of the 1840s the proud tribes of the North American Indians looked across the plains at the seemingly unstoppable expansion of the white man's West. During the decades of conflict that followed, as the new world pushed onward, the Indians saw their way of life disappear before their eyes. Over the next 40 years they clung to a dream of freedom and a continuation of their traditions, a dream that was repeatedly shattered by the whites.

Available at all good bookstores, or send a cheque to: **Pocket Essentials (Dept FM), 18 Coleswood Rd, Harpenden, Herts, AL5 1EQ, UK**. Please make cheques payable to 'Oldcastle Books.' Add 50p postage & packing for each book in the UK and £1 elsewhere.

US customers can send $6.95 plus $1.95 postage & packing for each book to: **Trafalgar Square Publishing, PO Box 257, Howe Hill Road, North Pomfret, Vermont 05053, USA**. e-mail: tsquare@sover.net

Customers worldwide can order online at **www.pocketessentials.com**